THE BEDFORD SERIES IN HISTORY AND CULTURE

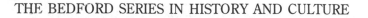

Jimmy Carter and the Energy Crisis of the 1970s

The "Crisis of Confidence" Speech of July 15, 1979

A BRIEF HISTORY WITH DOCUMENTS

Related Titles in
THE BEDFORD SERIES IN HISTORY AND CULTURE
Advisory Editors: Natalie Zemon Davis, *Princeton University*
Ernest R. May, *Harvard University*
Lynn Hunt, *University of California, Los Angeles*
David W. Blight, *Yale University*

The Age of McCarthyism: A Brief History with Documents,
Second Edition
Ellen Schrecker, *Yeshiva University*

American Cold War Strategy: Interpreting NSC 68
Edited with an Introduction by Ernest R. May, *Harvard University*

BROWN V. BOARD OF EDUCATION: *A Brief History with Documents*
Waldo E. Martin Jr., *University of California, Berkeley*

*Lyndon B. Johnson and American Liberalism: A Brief Biography
with Documents*
Bruce J. Schulman, *Boston University*

Jimmy Carter and the Energy Crisis of the 1970s

The "Crisis of Confidence" Speech of July 15, 1979

A BRIEF HISTORY WITH DOCUMENTS

Daniel Horowitz

Smith College

BEDFORD/ST. MARTIN'S   Boston   ◆   New York

For Bedford/St. Martin's

Executive Editor for History: Mary V. Dougherty
Director of Development for History: Jane Knetzger
Developmental Editor: William Lombardo
Senior Production Supervisor: Dennis J. Conroy
Production Associate: Chris Gross
Senior Marketing Manager: Jenna Bookin Barry
Project Management: Books By Design, Inc.
Text Design: Claire Seng-Niemoeller
Indexer: Books By Design, Inc.
Cover Design: Billy Boardman
Cover Photo: President Carter Delivers the "Energy and National Goals" Speech from the Oval Office, July 15, 1979. Courtesy of the Jimmy Carter Library.
Composition: Stratford Publishing Services
Printing and Binding: Haddon Craftsmen, an RR Donnelley & Sons Company

President: Joan E. Feinberg
Editorial Director: Denise B. Wydra
Director of Marketing: Karen Melton Soeltz
Director of Editing, Design, and Production: Marcia Cohen
Manager, Publishing Services: Emily Berleth

Library of Congress Control Number: 2004104019

For information, write: Bedford/St. Martin's, 75 Arlington Street, Boston, MA 02116
(617-399-4000)

ISBN: 0-312-40122-1
EAN: 978-0-312-40122-1

Acknowledgments

Acknowledgments and copyrights appear at the back of the book on pages 193–94, which constitute an extension of the copyright page.

Foreword

The Bedford Series in History and Culture is designed so that readers can study the past as historians do.

The historian's first task is finding the evidence. Documents, letters, memoirs, interviews, pictures, movies, novels, or poems can provide facts and clues. Then the historian questions and compares the sources. There is more to do than in a courtroom, for hearsay evidence is welcome, and the historian is usually looking for answers beyond act and motive. Different views of an event may be as important as a single verdict. How a story is told may yield as much information as what it says.

Along the way the historian seeks help from other historians and perhaps from specialists in other disciplines. Finally, it is time to write, to decide on an interpretation and how to arrange the evidence for readers.

Each book in this series contains an important historical document or group of documents, each document a witness from the past and open to interpretation in different ways. The documents are combined with some element of historical narrative—an introduction or a biographical essay, for example—that provides students with an analysis of the primary source material and important background information about the world in which it was produced.

Each book in the series focuses on a specific topic within a specific historical period. Each provides a basis for lively thought and discussion about several aspects of the topic and the historian's role. Each is short enough (and inexpensive enough) to be a reasonable one-week assignment in a college course. Whether as classroom or personal reading, each book in the series provides firsthand experience of the challenge—and fun—of discovering, recreating, and interpreting the past.

Natalie Zemon Davis
Ernest R. May
Lynn Hunt
David W. Blight

Preface

In late April 2001, when Vice President Dick Cheney delivered a speech on what appeared to be the first major energy crisis since the late 1970s, he remarked that "conservation may be a sign of personal virtue, but it is not a sufficient basis for a sound, comprehensive energy policy." In response, writers on the *Boston Globe* commented, "Conservation is not freezing in the dark. It is not Jimmy Carter putting on a sweater and talking about limits in America."[1] More than twenty years after the end of the Carter administration, this image of Jimmy Carter as a public scold who lamented the United States' spendthrift selfishness remains embedded in the American mind. There is no better source of this impression than Carter's "crisis of confidence" speech of July 15, 1979, officially titled "Energy and National Goals."

Popularly known as the "malaise" speech, even though when Carter spoke he did not use that word, this is not only his most memorable national address but also one of the most significant speeches any American president delivered in the second half of the twentieth century. In it, he confronted Americans in a way uncharacteristic of modern presidents, with profound questions about the relationship between public well-being and private consumption. In a broader sense, Carter's speech represented a culminating point in American politics that stretched back to the mid-1960s and pointed forward to the election of Ronald Reagan in 1980 and the conservative ascendancy that would mark the rest of the century. This speech, and the events surrounding it, underscore the continuing battle in the United States between materialism and restraint, between economic growth and environmentalism. The events of 1979 also highlight the politics of deadlock—between political parties, branches of government, and competing visions of America's future.

---

[1] Steven Syre and Charles Stein, "Don't Drill a Hole in Conservation," *Boston Globe,* 10 May 2001, C-1.

The materials in this reader focus on a series of topics that are of interest to students of history and politics. First, the documents highlight the difficulties a president has when he tries to rally the nation around an issue that he understands to be vital but that eludes most Americans, especially when the immediacy of the crisis fades. The problems Carter faced underscore the question of how it is possible to provide effective leadership when the news a president brings is negative and, moreover, hits people in their pocketbooks. Carter's presidency makes us ponder what happens when a political system wrestles with difficult issues at the same time the system itself is not working effectively. In this reader, the voices of Carter's opponents— both Republicans and Democrats—offer a dynamic sense of the major transformations in American politics of the era: the emergence of irreconcilable tensions within the Democratic party and the shift of power and national leadership to the Republicans. The pessimism of the 1970s, shaped by the end of the war in Vietnam, Watergate, and the energy crisis, set the stage for the Reagan administration.

Second, the documents in this collection, many of them from White House files, enable students to peer over the shoulders of the president and his advisers as they engaged in debates at a critical juncture in U.S. history. On one side stood the pollster and presidential adviser Patrick Caddell (and ultimately President Carter himself), who saw the energy crisis in moral and spiritual terms. On the other side were Vice President Walter Mondale and domestic policy adviser Stuart Eizenstat, who saw it in political and economic terms that affected people's wallets and votes but did not reflect their spiritual well-being.

Third, this collection of documents gives readers an in-depth look at an enduring tension within American politics—the way in which economic growth continually bumps up against limits imposed by the natural environment. The energy crisis of the late 1970s highlights issues the nation still faces today in energy and environmental policy, including conservation and increased exploration for oil. Moreover, these specific issues enable readers to examine more general issues of excess and self-restraint in consumer culture.

Fourth, this collection explores the challenges posed to the autonomy of a world power when it is confronted by the decisions of the oil producers in OPEC (Organization of Petroleum Exporting Countries), with all the national and foreign policy issues that these involve. Events of the late 1970s—including the Arab-Israeli conflict, the rise of Islamic fundamentalism, and the increasing importance of the political economy of Middle East oil—highlight some of the origins of problems that remain at the center of U.S. foreign policy today. In the 1970s, the cold war conflict with the Soviet Union shaped Americans' outlook on the world and their perception of these events, especially the rise of Islamic fundamentalism, and led policymakers to draw conclusions different from those they would make in the post–cold war world of the 1990s and beyond.

Finally, this book highlights the role of intellectuals in shaping national policy and the conflicts inherent in a situation where they counsel a president who takes their ideas seriously, especially when those ideas evoke a problematic, pessimistic vision of a nation in decline. Carter personally consulted and read the works of three of the nation's leading intellectuals—Christopher Lasch, Daniel Bell, and Robert Bellah. Their writings sounded warnings that some people (including the president) found powerful and others saw as problematic. A president's reliance on cultural critique in addition to political considerations raises questions about the relationships between ideas and actions as well as about Carter's judgment.

Jimmy Carter and the Energy Crisis of the 1970s: The "Crisis of Confidence" Speech of July 15, 1979 examines this speech, the context in which it was delivered, and the issues it raised. Part One provides a historical overview of the era and presents an analysis of the events leading up to Carter's address. Part Two, the documents, is organized into six chapters that present a wealth of perspectives on the energy crisis of the 1970s and beyond. At the center, of course, is the speech itself, reprinted in full in chapter 4.

Framing Carter's address, chapters 1–3 examine the political and socioeconomic context of the mid-1970s (chapter 1), the intellectual traditions Carter drew on in crafting his remarks (chapter 2), and the vital debates within the Carter administration over which direction to take in explaining the urgency of the energy situation to the American people (chapter 3). Chapter 5 explores reactions to the speech from a wide variety of perspectives, including the press (conservatives, leftists, environmentalists, and ethnic and religious groups), citizens, leading intellectuals, and political opponents. Chapter 6 explores how these events looked in retrospect, highlighting how, a quarter of a century later, major figures in American life, including consumer advocate Ralph Nader, Vice President Dick Cheney, journalist Thomas Friedman, and Jimmy Carter himself, fought over the issues this book presents: overseas control of oil and its impact on U.S. foreign policy, the trade-off between environmentalism and economic growth, and the role of presidential leadership in times of crisis.

Throughout this book, plentiful readers' aids will help students prepare for class discussions or writing assignments. Each chapter begins with an introduction that places the documents in their historical context, and every document is introduced with a headnote, giving instructors maximum flexibility for making assignments. The cast of characters following the table of contents identifies the major political figures referenced throughout the book. The appendix includes a chronology of events framing the energy crisis of the 1970s and Carter's "crisis of confidence" speech, a list of ten questions that will help students focus on the most important points raised by the readings, a selected bibliography that includes numerous suggestions for further reading, and an index.

ACKNOWLEDGMENTS

I wish to acknowledge all those whose help eased the completion of this book: Robert Bohanan and Keith J. Shuler at the Jimmy Carter Library; at Smith College, the Committee on Faculty Compensation and Development, Donna Divine, Rachel Goldstein, Helen L. Horowitz, and Molly Reynolds; Howard Gallimore of the Southern Baptist Historical Library and Archives; Steve Gillon of the University of Oklahoma; Char Miller of Trinity University; Dean Rogers of the Vassar College Archives; at Bedford/St. Martin's, William Lombardo, Patricia Rossi, Jane Knetzger, and Emily Berleth; Kimberly Hamlin at the University of Texas at Austin; Lynn Dumenil at Occidental College; Deborah Miller at the Minnesota Historical Society; Leslie N. Sharp at Georgia Tech; readers for Bedford/St. Martin's, especially Otis L. Graham Jr. at the University of California–Santa Barbara, Todd Kerstetter at Texas Christian University, Kevin M. Kruse at Princeton University, Chris Lewis at the University of Colorado–Boulder, and Bruce J. Schulman at Boston University. Some of the material in the introduction relies on Daniel Horowitz, *The Anxieties of Affluence: Critiques of American Consumer Culture, 1939–1979* (University of Massachusetts Press, 2004).

Daniel Horowitz

Contents

Illustrations

Cast of Characters

The following list of individuals includes the authors of the documents and important political figures referenced throughout this book.

Brock Adams Carter's secretary of transportation, whose resignation from the cabinet was requested shortly after the July 15, 1979, speech.

Menachem Begin Prime minister of Israel who agreed to the Camp David accords in September 1978.

Daniel Bell Professor of sociology at Harvard and author of *The Cultural Contradictions of Capitalism* (1976), who discussed his work at a White House dinner in the spring of 1979.

Griffin Bell Carter's attorney general, dismissed from the cabinet shortly after the July 15, 1979, speech.

Robert Bellah Professor of sociology at the University of California at Berkeley and author of *The Broken Covenant: American Civil Religion in Time of Trial* (1975).

Michael Blumenthal Carter's secretary of the treasury, dismissed from the cabinet in late July 1979.

Leonid Brezhnev Premier of the Soviet Union who, on June 18, 1979, joined with Carter in signing the SALT II treaty.

Jerry Brown Governor of California in 1979 and possible challenger to Carter for the Democratic presidential nomination.

George H. W. Bush Vice president under Ronald Reagan and president, 1989–93.

George W. Bush President, 2001–.

Patrick Caddell Pollster and political adviser to Carter; urged the president to emphasize the spiritual and psychological dimensions of the nation's problems.

Joseph Califano Carter's secretary of health, education, and welfare, dismissed soon after the July 15, 1979, speech.

Hugh Carter The president's cousin and a special assistant for administration in the White House.

Jimmy Carter President of the United States, 1977–81.

Rosalynn Carter First lady of the United States and influential presidential adviser, who served as a conduit for Caddell's advice.

Richard (Dick) Cheney Oil company executive, secretary of defense under George H. W. Bush, and vice president under George W. Bush.

William Jefferson (Bill) Clinton President, 1993–2001.

John Connally Contender for the Republican presidential nomination in 1980.

Stuart Eizenstat Carter's senior domestic policy adviser, skeptical of the wisdom of Caddell's advice.

Gerald R. Ford President, 1974–77, who unsuccessfully wrestled with the problem of how to control inflation.

Thomas L. Friedman Pulitzer Prize–winning author and writer of a widely read column for the *New York Times*.

Hendrik Hertzberg Presidential speechwriter who played a key role in drafting the July 15, 1979, speech.

Saddam Hussein Seized power in Iraq in 1979.

Lyndon B. Johnson President, 1963–69.

Hamilton Jordan Part of Carter's inner circle and one of his most trusted advisers.

Edward M. (Ted) Kennedy U.S. senator (D-Mass.) who challenged Carter's renomination in 1980.

Ayatollah Khomeini Islamic fundamentalist leader of Iran beginning in 1979, whose government cut off oil exports to the United States.

Christopher Lasch Professor of history at the University of Rochester and author of *The Culture of Narcissism* (1979), a book that Carter and members of his staff read.

Marshall Loeb Senior editor at *Time* who, as Carter prepared his July 15, 1979, speech, urged the nation to support policies that decreased dependence on OPEC.

Walter Mondale Vice president under Carter and the principal opponent of Caddell's approach.

Ralph Nader The nation's leading consumer advocate and Green party candidate for president in 2000.

Achsah Nesmith Presidential speechwriter under Carter.

Richard M. Nixon President, 1969–74, who in 1973–74 tried unsuccessfully to solve the problems of rising energy prices.

Mohammad Reza Pahlavi American-backed leader (Shah) of Iran until 1979, when anti-American Islamic fundamentalists forced him from office.

Esther Peterson Carter's special assistant for consumer affairs, who advised the president to keep consumers in mind as he formulated energy policy.

Gerald (Jerry) Rafshoon Coordinator of Carter's media efforts.

Ronald Reagan Critical of Carter's emphasis on the nation's "malaise," he defeated Carter in 1980 and then served as president, 1981–89.

Anwar el-Sadat President of Egypt who agreed to a bilateral peace agreement with Israel at Camp David in September 1978.

Kitty Schirmer Assistant to Eizenstat.

James Schlesinger Carter's first secretary of energy, who resigned in late July 1979.

Greg Schneiders Assistant to Rafshoon.

Walter Shapiro Presidential speechwriter under Carter.

Theodore A. Snyder Jr. President of the Sierra Club who wrote an editorial critical of the potential impact of Carter's energy policy on the environment.

Gordon Stewart Presidential speechwriter under Carter.

David Stockman Member of the House of Representatives (R-Mich.) during Carter's presidency and author of a 1978 article critical of Carter's energy policy; director of the Office of Management and Budget in the Reagan administration.

Alexis de Tocqueville Author of *Democracy in America,* which Carter read as he thought about what the nation faced in 1979.

Paul Volcker Appointed chair of the Federal Reserve Board in 1979 by Carter; played a key role in bringing inflation under control.

PART ONE

Introduction: Jimmy Carter and an Age of Diminished Expectations

President Jimmy Carter's speech of July 15, 1979, was the most important national address of his single-term presidency and one of the most revealing delivered by a president in the second half of the twentieth century. Prepared in response to the second major energy crisis of the 1970s, the speech raised profound moral questions about the nation's historic pursuit of an ever rising standard of living. To shape his argument, Carter relied on the writings of those who warned Americans against a selfish pursuit of affluence at a time in the nation's history when most Americans were struggling to balance their household budgets. An examination of the forces that affected this speech illuminates key elements of American history in the 1970s. Carter's address to the nation occurred at a pivotal moment in the history of American politics. Issues such as energy consumption and conservation, presidential leadership, the connection between religion and politics, the relationship between the White House and Congress, the trade-off between economic growth and protection of the environment, and the transformation of the major political parties all came into play. Moreover, the choices Carter made as he prepared the speech raise questions about the role of intellectuals in public life and about a president's reliance on their ideas, rather than primarily on political calculations. Finally, the speech illuminates the crosscurrents that influenced the relationship between the United States and the world community at a critical moment in international relations. The issues and the predicaments framing and informing Carter's speech were not passing anomalies. Rather, they reflect what it means for a president (and a nation) to wrestle with problems that ebb and flow but never entirely go away.

The years leading up to Carter's address were characterized by a series of events that had eroded much of the nation's confidence and by a failure of presidential leadership to deal with these issues. From one perspective, the speech can be understood as one of the final events in a long trail of stalled political momentum and troublesome economic developments. The speech itself, along with the events and ideas that shaped it, paved the way for Ronald Reagan's rallying of the nation around a commitment to smaller government at home and a renewed sense of power abroad. In many ways, Carter's difficulties made possible Reagan's success.

Upon entering the White House in 1977, Carter faced challenges that were not easy to address. Since the mid-1960s, events such as the war in Vietnam, the Watergate scandal, escalating inflation, and the first shocks of the energy crisis in 1973 had shaken the confidence of many Americans. His immediate predecessors—Lyndon Johnson, Richard Nixon, and Gerald Ford—had failed to tame inflation, fend off recession, control escalating energy prices, and restore American power abroad. Indeed, their policies had in many ways only made matters worse. For example, on the key issue of inflation that so fundamentally shaped the 1970s, Johnson had dramatically increased expenditures on the war in Vietnam without accepting the politically unpopular but economically sensible policy of raising taxes; Nixon had carelessly implemented (and then abruptly ended) price controls; and Ford had pursued deeply flawed attempts at building public confidence by proposing a Whip Inflation Now! (WIN!) public relations campaign that met with derision. Thus when Carter took office, he confronted a mounting and complex crisis that his predecessors had failed to resolve.

The energy crisis of the 1970s was the latest chapter in a long series of events and trends that had created for many Americans a crisis of confidence in their nation's future. The energy situation, and Carter's handling of it, intensified what one scholar has called "the crisis of competence" that had been building since the mid-1960s. Changes in the dynamics and structure of American politics limited

Carter's ability to provide effective leadership. The tragedies of Vietnam and Watergate had undermined presidential power and strengthened congressional independence. In the 1970s, both major parties were being transformed. Within the Republican party, the rise of the Sun Belt states in the American South and West provided a platform for Christian evangelicals and economic conservatives to challenge the relatively moderate leadership that had controlled the party for decades. Among Democrats, the definition of liberalism itself was changing and sparked a struggle between those (including the Democratic leadership in Congress) who advocated a full range of government social programs inspired by Lyndon Johnson's Great Society and those, like Carter (and later Bill Clinton), who believed that the era of big government was over. In addition, Carter faced the competing and difficult-to-resolve tension between key constituencies in his party— for example, newly insurgent environmentalists who wanted to moderate growth versus the traditionally loyal labor union members who wanted secure jobs.[1]

If what Carter faced domestically would test the skills of any president, what he encountered internationally provided challenges that were at least equal in difficulty. He bore the brunt of the ability of the oil cartel OPEC (Organization of Petroleum Exporting Countries) to influence the supply and price of a resource vital to America's economy. Continuing cold war tensions with the Soviet Union complicated responses to the turmoil caused by the Iranian revolution of January 1979 and more generally by the rise of Islamic fundamentalism throughout the region. The persistence of the Arab-Israeli conflict made the Middle East, with its vast reserves of oil, a region whose problems often appeared intractable. Although Carter made some headway on these issues, especially at the Camp David summit between Egypt and Israel in 1978, at other key moments he looked weak and bumbling in his handling of events abroad.

Yet if the origins of Carter's difficulties were historical, to a considerable extent he made matters worse. Politically tone-deaf, he often refused to compromise with the liberal wing of the Democratic party that dominated Congress, and he had difficulty communicating with the American people. At the same time, he failed to develop a fully effective White House staff and was unsuccessful in resolving the conflicting positions within his own administration—most notably the tension between pollster Patrick Caddell, who saw Americans mired in a spiritual crisis of their own making, and Vice President Walter Mondale and chief domestic policy adviser Stuart Eizenstat, who insisted that Americans faced difficult, practical problems that public policy and presidential leadership could solve.

Thus the failure of Carter's presidency needs to be understood in the context of a broad political crisis in American life. The troubled administrations of Johnson, Nixon, Ford, and Carter convinced many Americans that it was problematic to rely on government for solutions to persistent social and economic difficulties. Ironically, Carter understood the seriousness of the domestic and international situations, but he was unable to convey what he sensed to the American people. His solutions—live more simply and rely less on the federal government—lacked appeal to most voters. Not ready to give up the American dream of a rising standard of living, voters blamed Carter and what they saw as a government controlled by special interests. All of this created a political vacuum characterized by faltering presidential leadership, problems to which there appeared to be no solutions, and the nation's lack of confidence in itself to solve those problems. Into this vacuum came Ronald Reagan and the Republican party, with their vision of a new direction for America.

The intense and interlocking crises of the late 1970s provide a window into the intersection between politics, religion, international events, and economic forces. The issues Carter confronted throughout his presidency remain with us, despite more than twenty-five years of analysis and political solutions that have differed considerably from those he offered.

THE 1970S: A DECADE OF TUMULT AND TRANSFORMATION

The 1970s were a momentous decade in the history of the United States. Although Americans understand the 1960s and 1980s as distinctive periods, for many the 1970s remain either depressing or nondescript. In the words of one chronicler, it was a time when "it seemed like nothing happened." Yet the historian Bruce J. Schulman has convincingly shown that "in race relations, religion, family life, politics, and popular culture, the 1970s marked the most significant watershed of modern American history, the beginning of our own time." A number of trends characterized the decade, and in many ways the rest of the century. What one observer has called "The Fourth Great Awakening" involved a powerful religious and spiritual revival that transformed millions of individual lives and brought into local and national politics an insistence on using state power to make the nation adhere to moral standards.[2] The Sun Belt increasingly emerged into a position of political and cultural dominance. National commitments to public life and government power in the economy came under attack, as millions of Americans embraced an appreciation of the free market and private life and accepted individual liberation at the expense of restraint and civility.

Although it is possible retrospectively to see the decade as a transformative one, most Americans experienced the 1970s as a painfully wrenching period. The Watergate scandal that resulted in the resignation of a disgraced President Richard Nixon in August 1974, the inglorious exit of the nation from Vietnam less than a year later, and soaring inflation and energy prices throughout much of the decade turned the optimism of the 1960s into pessimism. These events instilled in millions of Americans a new sense of limits as to what they could expect as workers, consumers, and citizens. Deindustrialization, which saw the exportation of hundreds of thousands of high-paying jobs abroad (especially in the auto and steel industries), signified a series of important shifts. Japan, a nation the United States had defeated in World War II, emerged in the 1970s as a formidable economic competitor and in the process challenged American global competitiveness. Within the United States, jobs shifted from the Rust Belt (Northeast and Midwest) to the Sun Belt, from manufacturing to the service sector, and from union to non-union. Rising house prices and decreasing rates of home ownership, declines in productivity, and shortages of key goods made the lives of millions of Americans more economically difficult. Stagflation—the simultaneous combination of rising prices, high unemployment, and slow economic growth—seemed resistant to policy remedies. Inflation, sparked in part by increasing oil prices, rose to 11 percent in 1974 and unemployment to 8.3 percent the following year. After both figures subsided, they rose again: inflation to 13.4 percent in 1979, at a time when growth of the gross national product (GNP) was nearly flat, and unemployment as high as 7.8 percent in 1980. The rates of joblessness for African American and Latino workers were often twice the national figures. By 1980, the dollar was worth 40 percent of what it had been in 1967. In 1973, the income of vast numbers of middle-class and working-class American families reached a peak that it did not attain again for at least a decade and a half, with tens of millions of households experiencing diminishing real incomes. Although by the end of the decade, real GNP and the number of people employed were higher than in 1970, the economic troubles of the decade left tens of millions of Americans disoriented, depressed, and ready for change.

The politics and economics of oil, both nationally and internationally, played a key role in shaping the nation's experiences in the 1970s. In the three decades before 1979, the United States increasingly depended on oil imports, especially from Arab states in the Middle East.[3] In 1960, the United States imported 16.5 percent of its oil, a figure that doubled by 1973 and then increased to nearly 50 percent in 1977. For decades, Americans had relied on cheap energy, something its influence in the Middle East, but more importantly domestic reserves, had made possible. Indeed, until the late 1940s, America had been a net exporter of energy. In the ensuing decades, American energy use grew at a fast pace, a result of prosperity, cheap energy costs, and careless disregard for the preservation of natural resources. Yet ominous signs were there for anyone who wanted to see them. Price controls, put in place by President Nixon in 1971 to tame inflation, meant that the cost of oil in the United States remained well below world levels. A growing GNP and continued lack of conservation had increased the domestic use of oil from 5.8 billion barrels in 1949 to more than 16.4 billion barrels in 1971. Despite the discovery and development of oil in Alaska, stable or declining domestic production and reserves gradually had made the nation more dependent on imports, at the same time that exporting nations, especially in the Middle East, were becoming restive with American economic and diplomatic dominance.

By the 1970s, the nation's reliance on imported oil was beginning to give foreign oil producers unprecedented influence over the country's future. America's dependence on OPEC was troubling and part of a larger pattern. Prosperity had caused increasingly significant imports of goods from abroad, not only oil from the Middle East but also automobiles and electronics from Western Europe and Asia. The resulting balance of payments problem, caused by an excess of imports over exports, prompted the United States to devalue the dollar in 1971, an action that reduced the wealth and income of oil-producing states.

The consequences of all these changes became increasingly clear in 1973. On October 6, the Yom Kippur War broke out when Egyptian and Syrian forces, backed by the Soviet Union, attacked Israel. The United States had long been a supporter of Israel, a result of considerations that were at once domestic (the power of the Jewish vote in key states), humanitarian (commitment to democratic regimes and to survivors of the Holocaust), and international (the position of Israel as a bulwark against the Soviet Union in the Middle East). On October 17, as part of their long struggle to wrest control of the oil industry from Western corporations and in order to protest American support of Israel, the oil-rich Arab states halted sales to the United States and reduced output. The result was the first energy crisis—characterized by soaring energy prices (and the resulting rise in inflation and interest rates) and actual shortages brought home by long lines at gasoline stations. When the embargo ended, the price of OPEC oil had increased more than 350 percent.

In the meantime, America had become politically and economically deadlocked. Despite escalating energy costs, Americans had increased rather than decreased their consumption. The debate and political maneuvering of 1973–74 produced remarkably little, except for exhaustion and a sense that the energy crisis was not only artificially induced but also media hyped. Then between 1974 and 1978, there was a lull, a period when, in real dollars, the price of oil actually decreased and supplies were plentiful. In these years, the urgency about conservation and deregulation of prices diminished, and the calls to action had little effect. Neither of Carter's two predecessors, Republican presidents Richard Nixon and Gerald Ford, had made significant headway in solving the nation's energy problems. The Arab oil embargo had come at a high point in the Watergate drama, when Nixon was distracted by the effort to save his presidency and his reputation. The challenges of politics and leadership, plus the widely held belief that the crisis had passed, prevented Ford from attempting to surmount the considerable economic and political impediments to a solution.

AMERICANS CONTEMPLATE THE CONSEQUENCES OF CHANGED CIRCUMSTANCES

In response to the energy crisis, stagflation, and more generally to the sense that the nation had lost its bearings, those who shaped American public opinion reflected on some of the key issues that the threats to economic well-being had raised. In his widely read essay "The Me Decade" (1976), Tom Wolfe used irony to chart the narcissistic paths toward self-discovery and self-transformation that millions of Americans had embarked on. In *Two Cheers for Capitalism* (1978), the conservative commentator Irving Kristol asked whether the way affluence intensifies yearnings but ultimately leaves them unsatisfied was undermining the nation's stability. Those who glorified the freedom that unfettered markets brought, such as University of Chicago economist Milton Friedman, began to shape public opinion and public policy in the 1970s, with their impact dramatically more apparent in the 1980s. In contrast, Amory B. Lovins, in *Soft Energy Paths: Toward a Durable Peace* (1977), a book Carter read, spelled out an alternative to reliance on high levels of consumption, fossil fuels, and nuclear energy. A spate of books gloomily (and in many ways wrongly) predicted that problems with abundance were destroying the American dream, among them Fred Hirsch's *Social Limits to Growth* (1976), Robert L. Heilbroner's *An Inquiry into the Human Prospect* (1974), William Leiss's *Limits to Satisfaction: An Essay on the Problems of Needs and Commodities* (1976), Donella H. Meadows et al.'s *The Limits to Growth* (1972), William Ophuls's *Ecology and the Politics of Scarcity* (1977), and Lester C. Thurow's *The Zero-Sum Society* (1980).

Some observers actually welcomed the energy crisis as a catalyst that would help cleanse society of materialism and selfishness. Under the 1979 headline "Why a Depression Might Be Good for Us All," Dartmouth College political scientist Roger D. Masters asked, "At what point does the cost of continued economic wealth exceed the benefits? Wouldn't a major depression teach us the vital lesson that human life is more than physical comfort and a cost-of-living increase?" Masters was not alone. In 1980, John Tirman, another political scientist, welcomed austerity, because continually increasing consumption distracts people from spiritual goals, degrades the environment, undermines the stability of communities and families, and threatens the values of simplicity and caring. "What America *really* needs is more shortages," wrote *New York Times* columnist James Reston when Nixon in 1973 called for conservation in response to dramatic rises in oil prices and in OPEC's power. "We need to cut down, slow up, stay at home, run around the block, eat vegetable soup, call up old friends and read a book once in a while."[4]

Politicians and social scientists tried to devise policies to restore the work ethic, encourage savings, and lessen what they saw as unproductive consumption. Social scientists worried that self-indulgence undermined the fabric of American society and expressed concern about the dangers of profligate spending, both of the middle class and those below. Some observers detected a shift among Americans toward nonmaterial pleasures. In *New Rules: Searching for Self-Fulfillment in a World Turned Upside Down* (1981), the pollster Daniel Yankelovich described an emerging sense among Americans that additional material goods did not make them feel better. Rather, Yankelovich believed,

Americans sought deeper satisfaction in meaningful work, human relationships, leisure, community, and autonomy. Social scientists who carried out empirical studies that examined whether affluence made people happier offered sobering conclusions. In a 1973 article titled "Does Money Buy Happiness?" the demographer Robert Easterlin remarked, "To the outside observer, economic growth appears to be producing an ever more affluent society, but to those involved in the process, affluence will always remain a distant, urgently sought, but never attained goal." In 1978, sociologist Morris Janowitz reported that after 1959, increasing levels of income had not produced greater levels of personal satisfaction. Even as most Americans drove their energy-inefficient cars on superhighways and aspired to afford larger living quarters, E. F. Schumacher told people that *Small Is Beautiful* (1973), and the *Whole Earth Catalog* (1968) offered practical advice on how to live more simply.[5]

If some writers emphasized simple living, newspapers and magazines focused on what it meant for average American families to struggle to make ends meet. In March 1980, the *Los Angeles Times* featured a story about the Millers of Temple City, California, under the headline "Family Prunes Luxuries: On $25,000 a Year, No More Malted Milks." A reporter for *Texas Monthly* told the story of the members of the Mark Cunningham household of Plano, Texas, who sang "The $38,000 a Year, Wife and Two Kids, House and a Pool Blues." Howard J. Ruff's *How to Prosper in the Coming Bad Years* (1979), which by early 1980 had sold 500,000 copies in hardcover and more than twice that figure in paperback, warned people that since the nation's wealth was an illusion, they should put their assets in gold, buy a year's supply of food, head to small towns, and wait for better days when the free market might return the nation to sanity and economic health.[6]

In the 1970s, three of the nation's leading intellectuals wrote widely read books in which they chastised Americans for their excessive participation in consumer culture. In *The Culture of Narcissism: American Life in an Age of Diminishing Expectations* (1979), University of Rochester historian Christopher Lasch argued that mass consumption helped foster a new and dangerous self-indulgence (see Document 7). In *The Cultural Contradictions of Capitalism* (1976), Harvard sociologist Daniel Bell described a society coming apart because of the decline of the work ethic and the rise of self-indulgence. He asserted that religion would promote self-restraint and called for a renewed sense of the public good. In *The Broken Covenant* (1975), Berkeley sociologist of religion Robert Bellah urged Americans to draw inspiration from their national traditions so that they would turn away from excessive self-indulgence and instead embrace communal and ennobling virtues.

Lasch, Bell, and Bellah offered powerful, controversial, and deeply pessimistic critiques of America as a consumer culture, a nation they believed was threatened by excessive self-expression, as well as by the demise of religious traditions and a sense of public good. Although their analyses, politics, and solutions differed in important ways and did not go unchallenged, they shared a number of commitments. What one observer said of Lasch applies to some extent to Bell and Bellah as well: They combined "cultural conservatism with a politics of the left." They all believed that America's pursuit of endless (and mindless) affluence and self-gratification posed serious threats to personal and national well-being. As intellectuals, they were interested in their ideas having an impact and making a difference.[7]

In 1979, their moment came. Jimmy Carter, who shared with them moralistic attitudes about the negative effects of America's consumer culture, invited all three of them to talk with him about their writings. At the time, Carter was contemplating the consequences of the energy crisis for his presidency and for the nation. On May 30, 1979, Bell and Lasch had dinner and an evening of conversation with the president, First Lady Rosalynn Carter, two members of the president's staff (Jody Powell and Patrick Caddell), founder of Common Cause John Gardner, civil rights activist Jesse Jackson, *Washington Post* writer Haynes Johnson, former presidential adviser and well-known commentator Bill Moyers, and *Washington Monthly* editor Charles Peters (see Document 6). In the days when Carter was preparing his July 15 speech at Camp David, Bellah was among those whom the president consulted. Bell, Bellah, Lasch, and Carter hoped that the energy crisis would make Americans less narcissistic and self-indulgent, traits they connected to the excesses of affluence. This welcoming of adversity, commonly expressed by elites in the period, ultimately struck most Americans as wrongheaded. The writings of Bell, Bellah, and Lasch, as well as their interactions with the president, underscored the complications that occur when intellectuals enter the inner sanctum where public policy is being formulated. Their sophisticated jeremiads that called on people to repent of their sins now found echoes in the words of a president whose religious beliefs and political difficulties encouraged him to articulate his own version of a moralistic position on affluence. The economic situation, Carter believed, had persuaded millions of Americans (though hardly a majority of them) to take refuge in self-gratification, a proclivity that the president and the writers he consulted found problematic.

A PRESIDENCY AND A NATION IN CRISIS

Elected to the nation's highest office in November 1976, Carter began his presidency in January 1977. Rarely using his full name, James Earl Carter Jr., Jimmy Carter was born in Plains, Georgia, in 1924. Southern born and bred, he graduated from the U.S. Naval Academy with a degree in engineering in 1946, married Rosalynn Smith, and served as an officer in the Navy for seven years. After his stint in the Navy, Carter returned to Plains to run his family's peanut farm. He began his career in state politics in 1962, serving in the Georgia senate for four years. He lost his first bid for the governorship in 1966 but was successful four years later, in 1970. He served one term as governor of Georgia and in 1974 began his campaign for the presidential nomination of the Democratic party. A deeply moral and religious man, he told Americans that they deserved a government as good as the people it served. Appealing to core American values, he emphasized simplicity, dignity, honesty, and integrity. He sounded, simultaneously, like a preacher castigating his congregation, a populist railing against corrupt corporations, a reformer attacking the inefficiencies of government, and a white southerner sympathetic to the plight of disadvantaged whites and blacks alike.

Energy issues commanded remarkably little attention in the 1976 presidential campaign in which Carter defeated Republican president Gerald Ford. Yet shortly after taking office on January 20, 1977, he made the energy situation his primary focus. Soon after his inauguration, a major shortage of natural gas combined with severely cold temperatures nationwide to underscore the importance of a steady supply of fuel. After persuading Congress to enact an emergency natural gas bill, Carter turned to long-term solutions. His efforts to develop and enact an energy policy would prove to be the most persistent and troublesome challenge of his presidency.[8]

In early February 1977, Carter announced his commitment to comprehensive energy legislation and then appointed James Schlesinger energy czar. Because Schlesinger had served in the Nixon and Ford cabinets, Carter's appointment made clear his effort to turn energy policy into a bipartisan issue. He promised that Schlesinger, working in secrecy to avoid pressure from interest groups and members of Congress, would produce a national energy plan (NEP) within ninety days. In a televised speech on April 18, 1977, Carter announced his plan, stating that it involved the "moral equivalent of war" (see Document 1). A few days later, his administration introduced the NEP, comprising 113 different and in many ways conflicting initiatives. Congress quickly dismembered and then buried it. In August 1977, Carter signed legislation creating the Department of Energy and appointed Schlesinger the new department's first secretary. Over the next two years, however, his policy initiatives produced disappointing results.

In 1979, a second energy crisis was sparked by continued instability in the Middle East. The previous fall, riots in Iran had threatened the regime of Mohammad Reza Pahlavi, whom the United States had installed in 1953 to counter the nationalist and pro-Soviet leader Mohammad Mossadegh. As the shah's modernizing but brutal regime tottered, workers in Iran's oil fields, influenced by Islamic clerics, struck, bringing exports to a halt. His rule no longer tenable, the shah left Iran in January 1979, and the Islamic fundamentalist revolution led by Ayatollah Khomeini swept the country. Khomeini preached against Western values and denounced the long tradition of American dominance of Iran. But those who shaped American foreign policy, including the president, relied on misinformation about Iran and misread the causes of Khomeini's popularity, leading to difficulties in dealing with the situation. In addition, the Carter administration was distracted by the Arab-Israeli peace process, normalization of relations with Communist China, and negotiations with the USSR over the SALT II arms control treaty. The dramatic events in Iran, after Saudi Arabia the region's largest oil exporter, brought to power a regime opposed to modernization and underscored the danger of rapid social and economic development that the shah had undertaken with the aid of oil revenues.

Other OPEC nations, especially Saudi Arabia, increased production to pick up the slack caused by the strike in Iran, but growing consumption in the industrialized nations created a worldwide oil shortage. By late December 1978, OPEC's coordinated efforts to regulate prices and production had collapsed, and oil prices spiraled upward. In April 1979, Carter warned Americans that unless they strengthened their commitment to conservation, the nation's growing reliance on imported oil would have grave consequences. Having begun deregulation of natural gas prices in October 1978, the president also decided to deregulate the price of oil. This would allow the cost of energy to rise to the level paid in the rest of the world. In addition, he recommended a windfall profits tax—a levy on sudden increases in earnings—the proceeds of which would finance conservation (an anticipated by-product of higher oil prices) and alternative energy sources.[9] Here Carter faced a difficult dilemma: Decontrolling oil prices would lower the pressure on supplies but increase inflation. That the United States used more energy per capita than any other industrial nation, thus increasing demand and driving up prices, strained relations with its allies in Western Europe and Japan. Americans were learning painful lessons the hard way (see Document 4).

As with the first energy crisis of 1973–74, this event made many Americans realize that they were living in an age of limits. For the first time since the end of World War II in 1945, the nation no longer appeared to control its economic destiny. "The American Century," announced by Henry Luce, one of the founders of *Time,* just before America's entry into World War II, seemed prematurely over. Petroleum prices, which had fallen to $12 to $13 per barrel by late 1978, skyrocketed to $30 to $35 per barrel by early 1980. In the lull between crises, underlying energy conditions had not improved. With domestic oil production falling, interest in developing nuclear energy increased but immediately came up against regulatory, environmental, and safety concerns. To make matters worse, on March 28, 1979, an accident at the nuclear power plant at Three Mile Island near Harrisburg, Pennsylvania, resulted in the release of hundreds of thousands of gallons of radioactive water into local rivers, terrifying the nation and underscoring the dangers of nuclear energy.

On July 15, 1979, the third anniversary of his nomination for the presidency, Carter delivered his "malaise speech" to 65 million Americans, the largest audience he reached while in office (see Documents 16, 17, and 18). He evoked the image of a nation plunged into crisis by the excesses of affluence and suggested a comprehensive energy policy. He castigated his fellow citizens for their extravagance as consumers, even though millions of Americans had grown anxious about their ability to buy the goods and services they wanted and deeply pessimistic about the nation's future. A wide range of factors influenced the president's speech, from the demands of international and domestic politics to the conflicting advice of those to whom he listened.

Among the most important forces that shaped Carter's remarks were his religious convictions. Historian Leo Ribuffo has made clear that the president's Christian faith informed his response to affluence and to energy policy. A Baptist and born-again Christian, Carter was deeply concerned with issues such as the sin of pride, the limits on human power, and the role of morality in personal life and public policy. He worried about maintaining the line between his private faith and his public pronouncements. He struggled with humility and maintained an opposition to display and artifice. Here he drew on traditions that went back to the Reformation of the sixteenth century and continued to characterize those American Protestant groups that retained some connection to their humble origins. The president's cultivation of "a plain style," Ribuffo has noted, "reflected his private battle against pride," which in turn affected both his demeanor and his politics. When running for the presidency in 1976, he insisted on carrying his own garment bag. After taking the oath of office, he walked down Pennsylvania Avenue from the Capitol to the White House. He canceled special limousine services for leading staff members. He eliminated fancy tablecloths and seating in order of rank at the White House mess. Early in his presidency, he sold off the presidential yacht *Sequoia,* convinced that to the extent possible, a president paid by the taxpayers should not live with the trappings of wealth that almost all those who had elected him could not afford. Even while acknowledging the origins of Carter's religious convictions, one should note that his adoption of a plain style also reflected his development of a conscious and shrewd political strategy through which he hoped to sustain his image as an outsider and persuade Americans that he, too, was sacrificing private pleasures for the public good.[10]

The political and economic challenges Carter faced were formidable and would have been difficult to resolve under the best of circumstances. As a leader, Carter had a number of weaknesses that his energy policies revealed. He often adopted a high-minded rhetoric that struck many as patronizing or self-righteous. He had a penchant for moralizing and preferred speaking directly to the people rather than negotiating with Congress. He also was a stickler for detail, precision, and rationalism and insisted on comprehensive, all-or-nothing approaches to issues.

A number of factors undermined his policy initiatives, which focused on increasing domestic production of oil and decreasing consumption in order to lessen U.S. reliance on imported oil. Republicans, as well as Democrats from energy-rich states, favored increased production, while Democrats from the North fought for conservation. Rare, however, was the politician who would openly welcome higher prices. Complex government regulation of energy prices was difficult

Jimmy Carter working at his desk in the Oval Office, February 8, 1977.
Presidential photograph, #173610. Courtesy: Jimmy Carter Library.

to make simple or intelligible to most Americans. The bureaucratic situation was a nightmare, as several cabinet departments and at least five committees in each branch of Congress had jurisdiction over energy policy. Environmentalists and business interests fought over conservation measures, many of which would take years to have an effect. In addition, the ingrained habits of consumers, developed over decades of abundant energy supplies, hindered plans to promote conservation. OPEC acted as a powerful quasi-monopoly, with its ability to raise prices and control production making it difficult, if not impossible, to challenge. Although Carter's attacks on OPEC were good for domestic politics, they were problematic for the nation's diplomatic efforts abroad.

Rationing gas or oil would distort the market and anger users. Increasing taxes or decontrolling government-regulated prices would alienate liberals in the Democratic party (especially those from the North, where inexpensive heating oil was desirable) and affect those least able to pay. In addition, any combination of price decontrols, taxes on energy, and quotas on imports would fuel inflation and might drive the economy further into a recession.

As Carter spoke in July 1979, increasing signs of trouble for him and the nation were abundant (see Document 3). Inflation was running at a rate of more than 12 percent, with gasoline prices having increased 55 percent in the first half of the year. Lines at gas stations in California had begun to appear in April, as the nation's growing use of oil came up against limited supplies. In mid-1979, almost two-thirds of Americans reported to a pollster that the nation was in very serious trouble. Violence broke out surrounding a strike by truckers protesting rising gas prices. In June, Carter's approval rating slipped to the mid-20s, as low as Nixon's during the Watergate crisis. Higher prices, combined with gas shortages, sporadic violence over supplies, and long lines at gas stations, further hurt the popularity of the already-beleaguered president. By June 1979, an energy crisis equal in severity to that of 1973 engulfed the nation. A week before Carter's speech, 90 percent of the gas stations in the New York City metropolitan area were closed. In response to all these challenges, the president worked on developing an energy policy and an explanation of the situation in which the nation found itself.

PATRICK CADDELL AND
THE AMERICAN SPIRITUAL CRISIS

When Carter considered his policy and political options in 1979, the pollster and "intellectual gadfly" Patrick Caddell served as his primary adviser and the conduit for (and synthesizer of) the ideas that intellectuals such as Bell, Bellah, and Lasch had developed. Caddell, a Roman Catholic in his late twenties, was a maverick who had entered national politics as an undergraduate at Harvard, when he served as the chief pollster for George McGovern's 1972 presidential campaign in Massachusetts. The only non-Georgian in Carter's inner circle, Caddell commanded Carter's attention for several reasons. At critical moments, Rosalynn Carter eased Caddell's access to the chief executive. He caught the president's ear with arguments and statistics that alarmed Carter without offending or blaming him. He was aware of the president's perilous political situation without being immobilized or trapped by it. At the time, he had a reputation as a brilliant pollster and an innovative conceptualizer. Most important, he shared with Carter a sense that profound moral and spiritual issues lay at the heart of the crisis the president and the nation faced.[11]

On April 23, 1979, in response to Rosalynn Carter's suggestion, Caddell wrote a seventy-five-page memo to the president titled "Of Crisis and Opportunity." White House staffers termed the document "Apocalypse Now." Relying on his polling data, Caddell charted the diminishing faith Americans had in the president, the nation, and their futures. He asserted that long-term tendencies and factors, rather than the president's shortcomings, explained the crisis and provided challenges for him to meet. Looking forward bleakly to the 1980 election, Caddell ranged widely as he told Carter of the perils he faced and the opportunities they afforded him for leadership, which could turn him into a president of the stature of Abraham Lincoln or Franklin Roosevelt. Central to Caddell's message was the argument that Americans felt a "malaise" that signaled the depth of the nation's crisis. "Psychological more than material, it is a crisis of confidence marked by a dwindling faith in the future" that has especially affected the "better educated, wealthier and younger," he told the president. Caddell laid out the origins of the crisis—the assassinations of beloved leaders such as John F. Kennedy, Robert F. Kennedy, and Martin Luther King Jr., as well as Watergate, Vietnam, stagflation, skyrocketing energy prices, and the president's plummeting popularity in the polls. The result was growing disaffection from politics and government. On the horizon was a threat from Massachusetts senator Ted Kennedy, heir to the mantle of two assassinated brothers, who was deciding whether to challenge Carter in the 1980 Democratic primaries. Committed to an activist federal government to a far greater extent than was Carter, Kennedy opposed the president on key issues such as decontrol of energy prices, leadership style, and health care (see Document 30).[12]

In a paragraph titled "The 'Me' Generation," Caddell briefly summarized Christopher Lasch's *Culture of Narcissism*. Referring to Tom Wolfe's characterization of a generation, Caddell wrote that "it has become a cliché, as the country has turned increasingly inward. Personal gratification has replaced national involvement everywhere. Christopher Lasch has written a depressing, important best seller 'Narcissism in America'—the title [which Caddell got wrong] tells much." Caddell then went on to highlight other symptoms. "Spending as if there is no tomorrow," Americans lived for the present, no longer planned for the future, and took on more debt, all of which had "replaced the stable rock of steady, prudent future planning." Productivity and a lack of commitment to the work ethic had declined dangerously. Greed and "selfishness seems to predominate every-where," replacing "sacrifice," philanthropy, and a sense of national purpose. In his analysis of the challenge of affluence, Caddell mentioned political scientist James MacGregor Burns's *Leadership* (1979), including Burns's discussion of the psychologist Abraham H. Maslow's treatment of a hierarchy of needs. Burns cited Maslow's argument that once lower needs such as hunger were satisfied, Americans would turn, in Caddell's words, to "affection and belongingness." Caddell quoted an editor of *U.S. News & World Report* who had written of the boredom affluence produced. Caddell also mentioned a 1930 essay by John Maynard Keynes in which the distinguished British economist had emphasized that in the long run, the challenge of affluence called for a "return to some of the most sure and certain principles of religion and traditional virtue," including "that avarice is a vice, . . . the love of money is detestable, that those walk most truly in the paths of virtue and sane wisdom who take least thought for the morrow."[13]

After summarizing what he had read, Caddell concluded that the "structure of crisis" was due to the consequences of America emerging in the 1960s as "the first true leisure society." As Keynes had predicted, Caddell noted, this produced a crisis in which the nation had to ask itself "what is the nature, purpose, structure, and function of a post-survival society?" Leaders had to "define or transmit those higher unrealized needs" Maslow had identified. Unfortunately, Caddell argued, the political system "failed to address" them. "Rather, politics," Caddell wrote as he echoed what Lasch had argued, "has taken on the nature of a spectator sport," with the personalities of politicians looming larger in the decision of voters. "Single issue constituencies," rather than a commitment to the general good, Caddell noted, undermined the promise of "rough consensus democracy." The mass media, television especially, lessened the quality of political debate. With politics failing, in the end this "spiritual crisis" would "lead the society to turn inward, the spiritual bonds will weaken, and invisibly, the country will become intangibly but inexorably only a shadow of its former self."[14]

To solve these problems, Caddell called on Carter to seize the opportunity to become a different kind of leader. To do so, Caddell recommended that the president restore a sense of public good by strengthening traditional values rather than by campaigning for specific policies and programs. Among these virtues he included personal responsibility, "excellence in work, . . . [and] spiritual and moral value regeneration." What was needed, Caddell insisted as he echoed Bellah, was a commitment to a covenant, an agreement among community members, that would restore the nation's sense of purpose and national greatness.[15]

CONFLICTING ADVICE FOR A PRESIDENT

By early July 1979, the situation in the White House had grown dire. The energy crisis and Carter's own political situation had become so severe that they commanded his immediate and sustained attention (see Documents 10 and 11). On June 28, OPEC once again raised prices, bringing them to a level 60 percent above where they had stood in December 1978. On July 1, an exhausted Carter returned from a trip to Vienna, where he had signed the SALT II treaty with the Soviet Union, and from the Tokyo summit, where he had helped bring about an agreement among the seven leading industrialized nations to curtail their use of energy through 1985 (see Document 9). Nevertheless, his ratings in the polls continued to fall. In addition, his advisers were fighting over turf, strategies, and policies. Concern was growing that the energy crisis was producing a recession and preventing Americans from taking their summer vacations. Stuart Eizenstat, his domestic policy adviser, had recently warned Carter of a worsening situation. Referring to the domestic consequences of the energy crisis, he remarked that "nothing else has so frustrated, confused, angered the American people — or so targeted their distress at you personally."[16]

On July 3, Carter went to Camp David with Rosalynn, carrying with him a 107-page memo from Caddell. The next day, after reading Caddell's memo and a draft of the speech on energy he was scheduled to deliver on July 5, Carter canceled the talk, without explanation, something presidents rarely do. He made this decision at the urging of Caddell, who, aside from Rosalynn, was the only one to recommend that the president take this dramatic course of action. Vice President Walter Mondale and most of Carter's advisers thought that canceling the speech was a fundamental mistake that revealed his political weakness and ineptitude. Once the decision was made, however, some key aides saw opportunity instead of catastrophe. His communications adviser, Gerald Rafshoon, for example, quickly understood the public relations advantage of having the president hold a domestic summit at Camp David, a recommendation Carter accepted.

In his memo, Caddell called on the president to make a "break-through" by combining a dramatic speech with bold action. His reading had convinced him that material success had eroded the nation's sense of purpose. He referred to a number of writers, including Alexis de Tocqueville (see Document 5), for his notion of how religion provides a counter to the dangers of affluence, and Maslow, for his idea of higher needs. From Lasch, Bell, and Bellah, *New Yorker* political writer Elizabeth Drew commented, Caddell "drew confirmation of the theory that as people give up on the future they put more emphasis on immediate gratification, and that the pursuit of immediate gratification weakens values needed for the future—hard work, savings." Caddell focused especially on the consequences of the coming-of-age of the baby boom generation and the events of the 1960s, which had resulted, Drew said in a summary of Caddell's views, in a rejection of "religion and other older values." In the memo, Caddell called on the president to hold a fireside chat, followed by an address to Congress. He evoked Sidney Lumet's 1976 movie *Network,* in which a TV newscaster inspires citizens, frustrated by the energy crisis, to shout, "We're mad as hell and we're not going to take it anymore!" He called on Carter to make OPEC "a common enemy, but in action as well as rhetoric." Dramatic actions, he argued, would refocus the presidency and put Carter in a stronger position for the 1980 campaign. Caddell argued that "ONLY A RADICAL APPROACH WILL RALLY THE COUNTRY," something that a "breakthrough" could accomplish. He called on the president not only to address policy issues but also to use them as "THE DRIVING ENGINE OF VALUE RESTORATION, NATIONAL UNITY, AND NATIONAL PURPOSE." Americans, he believed, would be *"more willing to sacrifice more and suffer more if they perceive a purpose, an enemy, and an end goal to that pain."*[17]

Caddell proposed a broad range of programs. In a section on government policies toward oil companies, he wrote that *"energy provides the vehicle for confrontation of national interest over special interest"* and urged that *"we must be unsparing in hammering that point."* He also called for curtailed consumption, an area, he noted, *"where we can prove our resolve, unite our country, relearn values like sacrifice, unity, and send crucial signals to the world."* The central problem Caddell identified, according to Drew, was a "malaise" that had emerged because the United States "was a goal-oriented society without goals." In a handwritten letter to Caddell dated July 16, Carter called his analysis in the July discussions "a masterpiece."[18]

The president remained at Camp David for what turned out to be a week and a half, with July 6 through 13 taken up by the domestic summit. The press found his seclusion troubling. On July 6, the *New York Post* used a boldfaced headline to ask, "What the Heck Are You Up To, Mr. President?" In *Time* magazine, reporters wrote, "Rarely had a U.S. President seemed so mired in indecision." Carter left some of his key advisers in Washington, according to the newsweekly, and "baffled aides with almost nothing they could say for certain—except that the President had gone fishing." By July 6, people inside the administration began to take steps to reassure the public that the president was neither panicked nor confused. Rather, the word went out, Carter was consulting broadly as he focused his attention on the problems the nation faced.[19]

When it came time to turn discussions into a speech, Carter faced conflicting recommendations from within his administration, which Eizenstat characterized as involving "the most acrimonious debate" of Carter's presidency. The main disagreement surrounded the issue of whether the president should follow Caddell's suggestions that he scold citizens, call on them to restrain their consumption, and locate the larger spiritual and moral issues in Americans' selfishness and malaise. Eizenstat and Mondale saw the situation the president and the nation faced as having to do primarily with the practical, albeit formidable, issues of inflation, energy, and jobs (see Documents 9 and 13). Mondale had long but quietly dissented from Carter's policies and style. A Washington insider, he believed that Carter's inexperience with the ways of Washington and his status as an outsider had exacted considerable political costs. Moreover, as an heir of New Deal and Great Society liberalism, Mondale insisted that the Democratic party should support its constituency among working Amcricans in the North by focusing on issues such as health care, race relations, education, jobs, and housing. Criticized by his liberal friends and supporters for having traded access and position for influence, but loyal to the president, Mondale found himself in a difficult situation. In May 1979, he came close to resigning or at least deciding that he would not run again for vice president on a Carter-Mondale ticket. On July 4, standing in opposition to Caddell's approach, the vice president suggested that "instead of scolding the public we should play to their better instincts," sound an optimistic note, and offer pragmatic solutions to problems people faced in their daily lives.[20]

On July 5, recognizing how strongly his vice president felt, the president went for a walk with him on the grounds of Camp David, listening to his objections to Caddell's approach. Often joined in dissent by Eizenstat and Secretary of Energy James Schlesinger, Mondale told the president it was wrong to criticize Americans for being selfish and for suffering from a spiritual crisis. Mondale believed that Caddell had persuaded Carter to accept an approach based on half-baked psychological assumptions. Rather, Mondale believed, Americans were angry at government for failing to solve national problems and were struggling with objectively difficult conditions brought on by inflation, threats to job security, and exploding energy costs. The president should provide strong and bold leadership in solving what Mondale considered the real problems rather than deliver a castigating sermon. The battle was more than one between those who offered a broader analysis, such as Caddell, and those with more mundane political interests. After all, Mondale and his allies, including inflation adviser Alfred Kahn, themselves relied on the arguments of intellectuals, such as political scientist Theodore Lowi, who believed that interest group politics had fractured a sense of national purpose and as a result had paralyzed the political system.[21]

Opposition to Caddell also came from the White House communications office, headed by Gerald Rafshoon, a successful Atlanta advertising executive who had spearheaded the media efforts of Carter's gubernatorial and presidential campaigns (see Document 15). Joining Rafshoon was his assistant Greg Schneiders. Though differing in their approaches, Rafshoon and Schneiders continually warned Carter to act decisively rather than talk philosophically, academically, or apologetically. They were no less sensitive to issues of image than Caddell; indeed critics found them anti-intellectual and excessively focused on the media. Like Mondale, however, Rafshoon and Schneiders wanted Carter to avoid Caddell's emphasis on apocalypse and malaise and focus instead on action, decisiveness, and leadership.[22]

In contrast, Caddell called on the president to pronounce that the nation was in a crisis that was both spiritual and psychological. In a July 12, 1979, memo to Carter, Caddell summarized polling data that "signaled a rapid disintegration of optimism and efficacy in the country." This underscored the "increasing malaise" affecting the nation and the presidency. To bolster his case for a wide-ranging speech, Caddell reminded the president of the arguments writers had offered in their "INTELLECTUAL EXPLORATION." Lasch's book, he noted, examined how "people who lose sense of future turn inward for fulfillment which leads to vacuum and greater unhappiness," as well as a "loss of sense of meaning of life for future." Caddell also told the president about a recent newspaper article by Bellah, "Human Conditions for a Good Society," that "explored the loss of 'covenant' in the society" and "insisted that public confidence and commitment to the common good will destroy the conditions of freedom in society and precipitate the coming of tyranny" (see Document 8). Daniel Bell, Caddell asserted, "combine[d] much of Lasch and Bellah." He summarized Bell's *Cultural Contradictions of Capitalism* by emphasizing how "'modernism' and loss of faith," "much like narcissism," were "undermining the society." Caddell went on to emphasize the battle between "civitas" (the public good) and an increasing sense of entitlement. "Economic growth as secular religion," combined with inflation and a slower increase in the GNP, "leads to change in character of society making restraint, discipline and common interest almost impossible." This in turn leads to a situation where "values are weakened."[23]

Almost 150 people—representing politics, labor, business, religion, and ideas—talked to Carter at Camp David. The people he assembled included what was then an unusually significant number of women and African Americans, as well as more religious leaders than any president had previously consulted on policy issues. Every day, ten to twenty citizens joined the president and members of his staff in Laurel Lodge. They sat around a large conference table while the president conducted a series of wide-ranging meetings. Before the summit was over, Carter made surprise, and in many ways unprecedented, visits to two nearby homes. These trips enabled him to garner good press as well as to listen to ordinary citizens criticize him (see photograph on page 112).

Two decisions emerged from the discussions Carter orchestrated at Camp David. First, the president decided that he had to shake up and reorganize his administration. Such a solution would involve getting rid of cabinet members who were considered ineffective or not sufficiently loyal. Carter also realized that he had to straighten out lines of authority among his advisers, so that his administration could speak with a more consistent voice. Second, the talks at Camp David convinced the president that he should use his upcoming speech on energy to address the issues of the national spiritual malaise that Caddell had urged him to emphasize.

THE PRESIDENT ADDRESSES THE NATION

On July 15, President Carter delivered his address from the White House (see Document 18). His long stay at Camp David had created drama and mystery, heightening the sense of the speech's importance. Dressed in a dark suit, Carter sat at a table with American flags on both sides behind him. He kept his hands folded in front of him, sometimes moving them awkwardly to emphasize a point. His voice and animation increased at key moments, including when he noted that America was experiencing a crisis of confidence that struck at the nation's social fabric. The situation the nation faced, Carter asserted, was "deeper than gasoline lines or energy shortages, deeper even than inflation or recession." After confessing his own failures as a leader and giving examples of what he had heard during his retreat at Camp David, he focused on what he saw as threatening America: a "crisis of confidence" that had led Americans to doubt the meaning of their own lives, the future, and the nation's purpose, and as a consequence threatened "to destroy the social and the political fabric" of the nation. "Just as we are losing our confidence in the future," Carter remarked, echoing what Lasch had written about how Americans were increasingly cut off from their history, "we are also beginning to close the door on our past."

Carter located this crisis in many sources but especially in the tumultuous events of the previous two decades, which had set Americans on a pessimistic course. The results were evident. Americans had lost faith in their government and in their own ability to govern. Politicians had developed a greater obligation to special interests than to a common purpose. Americans had lost respect for key social and political institutions. Productivity, savings, and a willingness to sacrifice had decreased. To solve the energy crisis and the crisis of confidence, Carter held out the hope of getting the nation on the "path of common purpose and the restoration of American values." After suggesting policy initiatives, Carter reiterated his claim that solving the energy crisis could "rekindle our sense of unity, our confidence in the future, and give our Nation and all of us individually a new sense of purpose."[24]

Carter's speech operated on a number of levels and incorporated the conflicting advice his aides had given him. The first half of the speech reflected Caddell's emphasis on a national spiritual crisis, whereas the second half focused on the call of Eizenstat, Mondale, and Rafshoon for concrete policy initiatives. Confessing that he had failed the nation, Carter linked Americans' loss of confidence in him with their loss of faith in the nation's institutions and its future. Thus Carter made energy policy the test of the nation's ability to solve its moral and spiritual problems. As a born-again Christian, he delivered a sermon that relied on a Christian drama of retreat (to Camp David), a confession of sinfulness (his letting the nation down, along with the nation's journey into excessive consumption), a decision to commit himself and the nation to a battle against sin and for national recovery, and a claim of rebirth for himself and for America. Having asserted that Americans had fallen victim to self-indulgence, the president promised a new faith born of a cleansing and rededication—one that operated simultaneously on the political, religious, and personal levels.

Carter's speech involved what was surely the most sustained attack any American president had ever made on affluence. As Leo Ribuffo has argued, the speech was a jeremiad that "came as close to a call for a day of fasting and humiliation as any other modern presidential speech." One of Carter's most sweeping claims about the sources of what threatened America came when he focused on the consequences of affluence. He contrasted "a nation that was proud of hard work, strong families, close-knit communities, and our faith in God" with what he saw as its opposites. "Too many of us now tend to worship self-indulgence and consumption," he remarked. As a consequence, "human identity is no longer defined by what one does, but by what one owns." Ultimately, however, he felt this culture of consumption left Americans empty. "Owning things and consuming things," he noted as he emphasized the word *things* and his face made apparent his disgust, "does not satisfy our longing for meaning." Americans, he concluded, had learned that "piling up material goods cannot fill the emptiness of lives which have no confidence or purpose." From their presidents, Americans expect optimism and encouragement, not pessimism and chastisement, and although many Americans shared Carter's vision of moral consumption, most wanted to continue consuming, not be warned of the immorality of their pursuit of a good life. They sought acknowledgment of a crisis but not a substantial change in their way of life.[25]

Although the speech gave Carter a temporary boost in the polls, he was soon plagued again by low approval ratings, bad publicity, and political controversy. Two days after the speech, Carter began a major reorganization of his administration, reinforcing the perception that he was politically inept and that the government was in crisis. Instead of leading decisively by announcing changes, he asked his entire cabinet and all senior members of the White House staff to offer their resignations. Following this unprecedented step, he announced whose resignations he would accept. Since all cabinet and staff members served at the pleasure of the president, this was an unnecessary move. He then fired Secretary of Health, Education, and Welfare Joseph Califano, long protected by his close friendship with Mondale and by his earlier position in Lyndon Johnson's cabinet and as a proponent of the Great

"Who's In Charge Here?"
7/18/79

Herblock, *"Who's in Charge Here?"*
Reprinted with permission of The Herb Block Foundation. From *Herblock On All Fronts* (New American Library, 1980).

Society. Carter also accepted the resignation of Secretary of Treasury Michael Blumenthal, Secretary of Energy James Schlesinger, and Attorney General Griffin Bell. Of the four, Bell and Schlesinger genuinely wished to leave their posts. On July 20, the day Schlesinger departed, the president again blundered politically by awkwardly handling the dismissal of Secretary of Transportation Brock Adams. At the same time, he appointed the politically unpopular Hamilton Jordan as his chief of staff, who promptly undercut the president's decisiveness and competence by his own ineptitude when he asked staff members to fill out a silly self-evaluation form that quickly was leaked to the press.

Reorganizing his administration so soon after the energy speech and in the clumsy way that he did robbed Carter of the political momentum his talk to the nation had given him. News of the shake-up in the administration quickly eclipsed the overall favorable reaction to his speech. Soon after the speech, Carter appointed Paul Volcker head of the Federal Reserve Board. Volcker then initiated the painful process of wringing inflation out of the economy. In the short term, however, increasing prices and high rates of inflation engulfed the end of the Carter presidency. By the end of July, the president's approval rating had dropped again, even lower than it had been before July 15 and even lower than Nixon's rating when he had resigned as a result of the Watergate scandal five years earlier.

CONCLUSION

Events abroad and at home continued to cloud Carter's future, as did criticisms of him for emphasizing what he saw as the nation's malaise. The day after Carter's speech, Saddam Hussein seized power in Iraq. Later in the year, on November 4, 1979, Islamic fundamentalists in Iran seized the American embassy and took many hostages, offering to release them if the United States returned the shah to Iran to stand trial (which Carter would not do). Throughout the remainder of Carter's presidency, fifty-three Americans were held captive in Iran. Three days later, Ted Kennedy launched his much-anticipated challenge to Carter's renomination (see Document 30). In late December, the Soviet Union invaded Afghanistan.

By the summer of 1980, Carter had secured the Democratic nomination despite Kennedy's challenge, but he faced a formidable Republican opponent, Ronald Reagan. Carter's faltering approach to presidential leadership, his preference for technical solutions that involved reliance on the federal government, and his embrace of lower aspirations for the nation at home and abroad contributed to Reagan's victory. According to Reagan's pollster Richard Wirthlin, Carter "completely misread the perception of what people wanted a leader to be. He set us up with a perfect foil. [The July 15 speech] made him sound impotent. It was the most important political speech in the last four years." Speaking on the eve of the election, Reagan denounced those who said "that a great national malaise is upon us." And in October 1980, a writer for the *New York Times* noted that critics had nailed Carter "to a cross of malaise."[26]

In his campaign for the presidency and then while in office, Reagan offered an interpretation of the past and a vision of the future that were strikingly different from Carter's. Reagan's vision, over time, moved many Americans from disillusionment to high optimism. He refused to accept the notion that the nation had arrived at a new era of limits, and he used the failures of Carter and his predecessors to check inflation, end recession, and solve the energy crisis as proof that liberalism and big government were the cause of and not the solution to America's problems. Reagan stepped into the vacuum created by Carter's failures and called on Americans with a new vision of restoring the nation's strength at home and abroad (see Document 31). Though Reagan's approach created a tough set of issues different from the ones Carter faced, to most Americans by the early 1980s the crisis of confidence had ended.

NOTES

[1]James L. Sundquist, "The Crisis of Competence in Our National Government," *Political Science Quarterly*, 95 (Summer 1980): 183–208. For recent evaluations of the Carter years, see Herbert D. Rosenbaum and Alexej Ugrinsky, eds., *Jimmy Carter: Foreign Policy and Post-Presidential Years* (Westport, Conn.: Greenwood Press, 1994); Herbert D. Rosenbaum and Alexej Ugrinsky, eds., *The Presidency and Domestic Policies of Jimmy Carter* (Westport, Conn.: Greenwood Press, 1994), especially Marilu Hunt McCarty, "Economic Aspects of the Carter Energy Program," 555–70, and Ann Mari May, "Economic Myth and Economic Reality: A Reexamination of the Carter Years," 649–66. For material on the Carter presidency, see the Selected Bibliography at the end of this book.

[2]Peter N. Carroll, *It Seemed Like Nothing Happened: America in the 1970s* (New Brunswick, N.J.: Rutgers University Press, 1984); Bruce J. Schulman, *The Seventies: The Great Shift in American Culture, Society, and Politics* (New York: Free Press, 2001), xiv; Robert W. Fogel, *The Fourth Great Awakening and the Future of Egalitarianism* (Chicago: University of Chicago Press, 2000).

[3]For the statistics of oil use and imports, see Franklin Tugwell, *The Energy Crisis and the American Political Economy: Politics and Markets in the Management of Natural Resources* (Stanford, Calif.: Stanford University Press, 1988), 120. In addition to Arab producers, the major players in OPEC were Nigeria and Venezuela. Among the most

important sources of oil from outside OPEC were Canada, Mexico, the United Kingdom, Puerto Rico, and the Virgin Islands.

⁴Roger D. Masters, "Why a Depression Might Be Good for Us All," *New York Times*, 31 Aug. 1979, sec. A, p. 23; John Tirman, "Austerity as a Guide," *New York Times*, 9 Nov. 1980, sec. E, p. 19; James Reston, "Who Needs More Gas?" *New York Times*, 11 Nov. 1973, sec. E, p. 13.

⁵Daniel Yankelovich, *New Rules: Searching for Self-Fulfillment in a World Turned Upside Down* (New York: Random House, 1981); Robert A. Easterlin, "Does Money Buy Happiness?" *Public Interest*, 30 (Winter 1973): 10; Morris Janowitz, *The Last Half-Century: Societal Change and Politics in America* (Chicago: University of Chicago Press, 1978), 155. This paragraph also relies on David E. Shi, *The Simple Life: Plain Living and High Thinking in American Culture* (New York: Oxford University Press, 1985), 266–72.

⁶Sue Avery, "Family Prunes Luxuries: On $25,000 a Year, No More Malted Milks," *Los Angeles Times*, 2 Mar. 1980, sec. 12, p. 1; Michael Ennis, "The $38,000 a Year, Wife and Two Kids, House and a Pool *Blues*," *Texas Monthly*, Sept. 1980, 134; Howard J. Ruff, *How to Prosper in the Coming Bad Years* (New York: Times Books, 1979).

⁷Dennis H. Wrong, "Bourgeois Values, No Bourgeoisie? The Cultural Criticism of Christopher Lasch," *Dissent*, 26 (Summer 1979): 313.

⁸For an excellent discussion of Carter's energy policy, see John C. Barrow, "An Age of Limits: Jimmy Carter and the Quest for a National Policy," in *The Carter Presidency: Policy Choices in the Post–New Deal Era*, ed. Gary M. Fink and Hugh Davis Graham (Lawrence: University Press of Kansas, 1998), 158–78.

⁹Robert Stobaugh and Daniel Yergin, "Energy: An Emergency Telescoped," *Foreign Affairs*, 58 (1980): 563–95.

¹⁰Leo P. Ribuffo, "God and Jimmy Carter," in *Right Left Center: Essays in American History* (New Brunswick, N.J.: Rutgers University Press, 1992), 228. Among the most helpful discussions of the speech are Leo Ribuffo, "'Malaise' Revisited: Jimmy Carter and the Crisis of Confidence," in *The Liberal Persuasion: Arthur Schlesinger, Jr., and the Challenge of the American Past*, ed. John Patrick Diggins (Princeton, N.J.: Princeton University Press, 1997), 164–84, and J. William Holland, "The Great Gamble: Jimmy Carter and the 1979 Energy Crisis," *Prologue*, 22 (Spring 1990): 63–79. For other commentaries, see Kenneth E. Morris, *Jimmy Carter: American Moralist* (Athens: University of Georgia Press, 1996), 1–19, 251–62; Robert A. Strong, "Reclaiming Leadership: The Carter Administration and the Crisis of Confidence," *Political Science Quarterly*, 16 (Fall 1986): 636–50; Dan F. Hahn, "Flailing the Profligate: Carter's Energy Sermon of 1979," *Political Science Quarterly*, 10 (Fall 1980): 583–87; Elizabeth Drew, "A Reporter at Large: Phase—In Search of a Definition," *New Yorker*, 27 Aug. 1979, 45–46, 49–50, 53–54, 56, 59–60, 63–64, 66–73; Hedrick Smith, "Remaking of Carter's Presidency: 16 Days of Shifts and Reappraisals," *New York Times*, 22 July 1979, 1, 30; Hendrik Hertzberg, "Jimmy Carter, 1977–1981," in *Character Above All: Ten Presidents from FDR to George Bush*, ed. Robert A. Wilson (New York: Simon and Schuster, 1995), 190–94; Scott Kramer, "Struggles of an Outsider: The 1979 Energy Crisis and President Carter's Call for Confidence" (senior thesis, Department of History, Princeton University, 1992, copy in Jimmy Carter Presidential Library, Atlanta, Ga. [hereafter cited as JCPL]). In *Jimmy Carter*, Morris places the energy crisis; Carter's morality; the July 15, 1979, speech; and the malaise of the 1970s at the center of his analysis: see especially 1–19 and 240–88. For background information on the Carter presidency, see the Selected Bibliography at the end of this book.

¹¹Playboy Interview, "Pat Caddell," *Playboy*, Feb. 1980, 68.

¹²Patrick Caddell to Jimmy Carter, Memorandum, "Of Crisis and Opportunity," 23 Apr. 1979, Presidential Files: Jody Powell, box 40, folder "Memoranda: President Carter 1/10/79–4/23/79," JCPL, 1, 11. On Kennedy's relationship with Carter, see Adam Clymer, *Edward M. Kennedy: A Biography* (New York: William Morrow, 1999), 279–85.

[13]Caddell, "Of Crisis and Opportunity," 25, 26, 32–33; Marvin Stone, editorial comment, *U.S. News & World Report,* 5 Feb. 1979, quoted ibid., 27; John Maynard Keynes, quoted ibid., 35.

[14]Caddell, "Of Crisis and Opportunity," 36, 40, 49, 51, 59.

[15]Ibid., 66, 70.

[16]Stuart Eizenstat to Jimmy Carter, Memorandum, 28 June 1979, Office of Staff Secretary: Presidential Handwriting File, box 137, folder "Trip to Japan and Korea, 6/22/79–7/1/79 [1]," JCPL.

[17]Drew, "A Reporter at Large," 56; [Patrick Caddell], Memorandum [breakthrough memo], n.d. [probably late June or early July 1979], White House Central File: Utilities, box UT-1, folder "UT 5/19/79–1/20/81," JCPL, 49–50.

[18][Caddell], [breakthrough memo], 49–51, 53, 54; Jimmy Carter, Speech to Communications Workers of America, 16 July 1979, quoted in Drew, "A Reporter at Large," 56; Jimmy Carter to Patrick Caddell, Memorandum, 16 July 1979, Office of Staff Secretary: Presidential Handwriting File, box 139, folder "7/16/79 [2]," JCPL.

[19]*New York Post* headline quoted in Kramer, "Struggles," 87; "Carter Was Speechless," *Time,* 16 July 1979, 8.

[20]Walter Mondale to Jimmy Carter, Memorandum, 4 July 1979, Walter Mondale Papers, Minnesota Historical Society, quoted in Steven M. Gillon, *The Democrats' Dilemma: Walter F. Mondale and the Liberal Legacy* (New York: Columbia University Press, 1992), 261. This discussion of Mondale relies on Gillon, 251–66, and on Peter G. Bourne, *Jimmy Carter: A Comprehensive Biography from Plains to Postpresidency* (New York: Scribner, 1997), 441–44.

[21]Stuart Eizenstat, Interview, 29–30 Jan. 1982, Miller Center Interviews, box 1, JCPL, 80.

[22]Greg Schneiders to Gerald Rafshoon, Memorandum, 10 July 1979, Rafshoon Collection, box 28, folder "Memoranda from Jerry Rafshoon—June, July, August 1979," JCPL, 1–2; Gerald Rafshoon to Jimmy Carter, Memorandum, 10 July 1979, Speechwriters: Chronological File, box 50, folder "7/15/79 Address to the Nation—Energy/Crisis of Confidence [1]," JCPL, 1.

[23]Patrick Caddell to Jimmy Carter, Memorandum, 12 July 1979, Office of Staff Secretary: Presidential Handwriting File, box 138, folder "Camp David 7/5/79–7/12/79 [6]," JCPL, 1, 3–4.

[24]Jimmy Carter, "Energy and National Goals," 15 July 1979, *Public Papers of the Presidents of the United States: Jimmy Carter, 1977–81* (Washington, D.C.: Government Printing Office, 1980), 2:1235, 1237, 1238, 1240.

[25]Ribuffo, "God and Jimmy Carter," 240; Carter, "Energy," 1237.

[26]Richard Wirthlin, quoted in Robert Shogan, "Discussant," in *Jimmy Carter: Foreign Policy and Post-Presidential Years,* ed. Herbert D. Rosenbaum and Alexej Ugrinsky (Westport, Conn.: Greenwood Press, 1994), 394–95; Ronald Reagan, "A Vision for America," Television Address, 3 Nov. 1980, news release of same date, Ronald Reagan Library, Simi Valley, Calif.; Francis X. Clines, "Candidates Also Appeal to Those Basic Virtues," *New York Times,* 26 Oct. 1980, sec. E, p. 2.

PART TWO

The Documents

1

Carter Declares Energy Crisis the "Moral Equivalent of War"

The first two documents—President Jimmy Carter's first major address on energy and Congressman David Stockman's response—capture many of the essential elements of the wider debates that reverberated throughout the nation from 1973 until well into the 1980s. They bring together two opposing views of the energy crisis, of political leadership, and of the role of the federal government in the economy.

Shortly after taking office in January 1977, Carter delivered the first of his many energy messages. Calling the challenges the nation faced the "moral equivalent of war," he used dire predictions to shock Americans out of what he saw as the complacency that had overtaken them once the problems of the 1973 energy crisis had begun to fade. To provide hope in a situation he saw as potentially desperate, he called for action that placed government authority at the center of "an effective and comprehensive energy policy."

When he spoke to the nation on April 18, 1977, and then delivered a legislative package a few days later, Carter was making good on a promise he had articulated shortly after taking office less than three months before. Carter's speech and the 113 proposals he submitted to Congress reflect his commitment to a moral vision and a comprehensive set of solutions. He was trying to teach Americans that they had to make a transition from cheap energy that could be easily wasted without an awareness of international consequences to a use of energy that acknowledged the importance of conservation and the environment and the diplomatic implications of OPEC's power. Carter relied here on the work of his chief energy adviser, James Schlesinger, who had put together a national energy plan (NEP) that rested on often conflicting goals: the importance of conservation, greater reliance on coal, reduced levels of oil imports, stewardship of the natural environment, government-sponsored research into alternative sources, and (despite Carter's commitment during the 1976 campaign to end regulation) elaborate regulatory schemes that over time would increase oil and natural gas prices to world levels.

The results of Carter's speech and proposals were not what he had hoped for. Several factors undermined his political effectiveness. In the period between the end of the OPEC oil embargo of 1973 and the second energy crisis of 1979, many Americans had come to believe that the energy situation had improved and that the crisis had ended, a sentiment many legislators echoed. The president, whose instincts combined an engineer's rationality and a Baptist's morality, learned the hard way about how fiercely competing interest groups will fight over national policy. Without a crisis immediately at hand, it took the Senate six months and seventy-seven votes on five different bills to reach a consensus. Finally, in October 1978, the two houses of Congress came to an agreement. Although Carter signed the legislation, he hardly got what he wanted. For example, Congress had not adopted the central elements of his plan to conserve energy. His approval rating continued to sink, and many in Congress and the press blamed him for the failure to solve the nation's energy problems.

Carter failed to achieve the goals he set out in his speech for several reasons. He was often politically inept. In addition, he faced stiff opposition from the business community and conservatives, who doubted that the nation faced a situation as dire as Carter predicted. Moreover, these opponents believed that solutions would come if the government allowed markets to operate efficiently. David Stockman's "The Wrong War? The Case against a National Energy Policy," published a year and a half after Carter's speech, made the case against government intervention and for efficient markets.

Born in 1946 and a graduate of Michigan State University, Stockman was elected to Congress in 1976 as a Republican from Michigan. His analysis appeared in the Fall 1978 issue of *Public Interest,* a leading moderately conservative journal. When Ronald Reagan practiced for the 1980 presidential debates, Stockman role-played Jimmy Carter and the independent candidate John Anderson. He greatly impressed Reagan, who selected Stockman, still in his early thirties, as director of the Office of Management and Budget. Especially in the early days of the Reagan administration, Stockman used the skills so evident in this essay—his command of detail, his ease with economic statistics, and his commitment to a market economy in which the government played a minimal role—to reinforce the reorientation of the nation's priorities.

Stockman dissented from many of the premises of Carter's speech. He did not believe that the energy crisis was unprecedented, that the nation had to wean itself from a reliance on oil (especially imported oil), or that to do so the United States had to embrace federal government planning. In contrast, he insisted on the power of unfettered global markets to provide abundant energy. Stockman thus countered Carter's emphasis on stewardship, morality, and a comprehensive government program. Instead, he celebrated the ability of free markets to solve complicated problems such as those surrounding the provision of a steady flow of energy to the nation.

Stockman's essay reflects the growth in conservative ideology that was evident in Senator Barry Goldwater's 1964 presidential campaign, in the writings of the University of Chicago economist Milton Friedman (*Capitalism and Freedom,* 1962), and in Ronald Reagan's California governorship from 1967 to 1975. After the late 1960s, as the New Deal coalition fractured and faith in the efficacy of federal power diminished, people who advocated free markets and opposed federal intervention in the economy increasingly came into prominence. Stockman's essay pointed toward the approach to national economic problems that Reagan would bring to the White House in 1981—a faith in the American economy, a belief that centralized planning by the federal government only made matters worse, and the confidence that free markets would ensure abundant energy and a rising standard of living.

With the debate over the issues Carter and Stockman had raised in 1977 and 1978 unresolved, the energy crisis returned with full force in 1979. With OPEC continuing to raise prices and with the Islamic fundamentalist government in Iran cutting off shipments of oil to the United States, supplies became scarcer and prices resumed their rapid ascent. *Newsweek*'s July 2, 1979, article "The Energy Plague" chronicles the dramatic events that Carter faced upon his return to the United States from diplomatic triumphs abroad. People waited in long lines to get gas for their cars. Truckers went on strike to pressure the government to provide them with adequate supplies of fuel. Produce rotted in warehouses because trucks could not get it to markets. Events like these shook the confidence of Americans during Carter's presidency. In addition, as the editorial "Carter on the *Titanic*" from the *National Review* makes clear, the president faced determined opposition from many quarters, most importantly conservatives.

1

JIMMY CARTER

The Energy Problem

April 18, 1977

Less than three months after taking office, Carter delivered the first of his many energy messages. He used dire predictions to shock Americans out of what he saw as the complacency that had overtaken them and made government action central to the solution of the nation's energy problems.

Good evening.

Tonight I want to have an unpleasant talk with you about a problem that is unprecedented in our history. With the exception of preventing war, this is the greatest challenge that our country will face during our lifetime.

The energy crisis has not yet overwhelmed us, but it will if we do not act quickly. It's a problem that we will not be able to solve in the next few years, and it's likely to get progressively worse through the rest of this century.

We must not be selfish or timid if we hope to have a decent world for our children and our grandchildren. We simply must balance our demand for energy with our rapidly shrinking resources. By acting now we can control our future instead of letting the future control us.

Two days from now, I will present to the Congress my energy proposals. Its Members will be my partners, and they have already given me a great deal of valuable advice.

Many of these proposals will be unpopular. Some will cause you to put up with inconveniences and to make sacrifices. The most important thing about these proposals is that the alternative may be a national catastrophe. Further delay can affect our strength and our power as a nation.

Note: Throughout the documents, spelling and punctuation errors have been silently corrected.

Jimmy Carter, "The Energy Problem," 18 Apr. 1977, *Public Papers of the Presidents of the United States: Jimmy Carter, 1977–81* (Washington, D.C.: Government Printing Office, 1977), 1:656–62.

Our decision about energy will test the character of the American people and the ability of the President and the Congress to govern this Nation. This difficult effort will be the "moral equivalent of war,"[1] except that we will be uniting our efforts to build and not to destroy.

Now, I know that some of you may doubt that we face real energy shortages. The 1973 gas lines are gone, and with this springtime weather, our homes are warm again. But our energy problem is worse tonight than it was in 1973 or a few weeks ago in the dead of winter. It's worse because more waste has occurred and more time has passed by without our planning for the future. And it will get worse every day until we act.

The oil and natural gas that we rely on for 75 percent of our energy are simply running out. In spite of increased effort, domestic production has been dropping steadily at about 6 percent a year. Imports have doubled in the last 5 years. Our Nation's economic and political independence is becoming increasingly vulnerable. Unless profound changes are made to lower oil consumption, we now believe that early in the 1980s the world will be demanding more oil than it can produce.

The world now uses about 60 million barrels of oil a day, and demand increases each year about 5 percent. This means that just to stay even we need the production of a new Texas every year, an Alaskan North Slope every 9 months, or a new Saudi Arabia every 3 years. Obviously, this cannot continue.

We must look back into history to understand our energy problem. Twice in the last several hundred years, there has been a transition in the way people use energy.

The first was about 200 years ago, when we changed away from wood—which had provided about 90 percent of all fuel—to coal, which was much more efficient. This change became the basis of the Industrial Revolution.

The second change took place in this century, with the growing use of oil and natural gas. They were more convenient and cheaper than coal, and the supply seemed to be almost without limit. They made possible the age of automobile and airplane travel. Nearly everyone who is alive today grew up during this period, and we have never known anything different.

---

[1]In 1906, the philosopher and psychologist William James used "the moral equivalent of war" to describe how nonmilitary choices might foster the positive qualities that war encouraged in an overly comfortable nation.

Because we are now running out of gas and oil, we must prepare quickly for a third change—to strict conservation and to the renewed use of coal and to permanent renewable energy sources like solar power.

The world has not prepared for the future. During the 1950s, people used twice as much oil as during the 1940s. During the 1960s, we used twice as much as during the 1950s. And in each of those decades, more oil was consumed than in all of man's previous history combined.

World consumption of oil is still going up. If it were possible to keep it rising during the 1970s and 1980s by 5 percent a year, as it has in the past, we could use up all the proven reserves of oil in the entire world by the end of the next decade.

I know that many of you have suspected that some supplies of oil and gas are being withheld from the market. You may be right, but suspicions about the oil companies cannot change the fact that we are running out of petroleum.

All of us have heard about the large oil fields on Alaska's North Slope. In a few years, when the North Slope is producing fully, its total output will be just about equal to 2 years' increase in our own Nation's energy demand.

Each new inventory of world oil reserves has been more disturbing than the last. World oil production can probably keep going up for another 6 or 8 years. But sometime in the 1980s, it can't go up any more. Demand will overtake production. We have no choice about that.

But we do have a choice about how we will spend the next few years. Each American uses the energy equivalent of 60 barrels of oil per person each year. Ours is the most wasteful nation on Earth. We waste more energy than we import. With about the same standard of living, we use twice as much energy per person as do other countries like Germany, Japan, and Sweden.

One choice, of course, is to continue doing what we've been doing before. We can drift along for a few more years.

Our consumption of oil would keep going up every year. Our cars would continue to be too large and inefficient. Three-quarters of them would carry only one person—the driver—while our public transportation system continues to decline. We can delay insulating our homes, and they will continue to lose about 50 percent of their heat in waste. We can continue using scarce oil and natural gas to generate electricity and continue wasting two-thirds of their fuel value in the process.

If we do not act, then by 1985 we will be using 33 percent more energy than we use today.

We can't substantially increase our domestic production, so we would need to import twice as much oil as we do now. Supplies will be uncertain. The cost will keep going up. Six years ago, we paid $3.7 billion for imported oil. Last year we spent $36 billion for imported oil—nearly 10 times as much. And this year we may spend $45 billion.

Unless we act, we will spend more than $550 billion for imported oil by 1985—more than $2,500 for every man, woman, and child in America. Along with that money that we transport overseas, we will continue losing American jobs and become increasingly vulnerable to supply interruptions.

Now we have a choice. But if we wait, we will constantly live in fear of embargoes. We could endanger our freedom as a sovereign nation to act in foreign affairs. Within 10 years, we would not be able to import enough oil from any country, at any acceptable price.

If we wait and do not act, then our factories will not be able to keep our people on the job with reduced supplies of fuel.

Too few of our utility companies will have switched to coal, which is our most abundant energy source. We will not be ready to keep our transportation system running with smaller and more efficient cars and a better network of buses, trains, and public transportation.

We will feel mounting pressure to plunder the environment. We will have to have a crash program to build more nuclear plants, strip mine and burn more coal, and drill more offshore wells than if we begin to conserve right now.

Inflation will soar; production will go down; people will lose their jobs. Intense competition for oil will build up among nations and also among the different regions within our own country. This has already started.

If we fail to act soon, we will face an economic, social, and political crisis that will threaten our free institutions. But we still have another choice. We can begin to prepare right now. We can decide to act while there is still time. That is the concept of the energy policy that we will present on Wednesday.

Our national energy plan is based on 10 fundamental principles. The first principle is that we can have an effective and comprehensive energy policy only if the Government takes responsibility for it and if the people understand the seriousness of the challenge and are willing to make sacrifices.

The second principle is that healthy economic growth must continue.

Only by saving energy can we maintain our standard of living and keep our people at work. An effective conservation program will create hundreds of thousands of new jobs.

The third principle is that we must protect the environment. Our energy problems have the same cause as our environmental problems— wasteful use of resources. Conservation helps us solve both problems at once.

The fourth principle is that we must reduce our vulnerability to potentially devastating embargoes. We can protect ourselves from uncertain supplies by reducing our demand for oil, by making the most of our abundant resources such as coal, and by developing a strategic petroleum reserve.

The fifth principle is that we must be fair. Our solutions must ask equal sacrifices from every region, every class of people, and every interest group. Industry will have to do its part to conserve just as consumers will. The energy producers deserve fair treatment, but we will not let the oil companies profiteer.

The sixth principle, and the cornerstone of our policy, is to reduce demand through conservation. Our emphasis on conservation is a clear difference between this plan and others which merely encouraged crash production efforts. Conservation is the quickest, cheapest, most practical source of energy. Conservation is the only way that we can buy a barrel of oil for about $2. It costs about $13 to waste it.

The seventh principle is that prices should generally reflect the true replacement cost of energy. We are only cheating ourselves if we make energy artificially cheap and use more than we can really afford.

The eighth principle is that Government policies must be predictable and certain. Both consumers and producers need policies they can count on so they can plan ahead. This is one reason that I'm working with the Congress to create a new Department of Energy to replace more than 50 different agencies that now have some control over energy.

The ninth principle is that we must conserve the fuels that are scarcest and make the most of those that are plentiful. We can't continue to use oil and gas for 75 percent of our consumption, as we do now, when they only make up 7 percent of our domestic reserves. We need to shift to plentiful coal, while taking care to protect the environment, and to apply stricter safety standards to nuclear energy.

The tenth and last principle is that we must start now to develop the new, unconventional sources of energy that we will rely on in the next century.

Now, these 10 principles have guided the development of the policy that I will describe to you and the Congress on Wednesday night.

Our energy plan will also include a number of specific goals to measure our progress toward a stable energy system. These are the goals that we set for 1985:

—to reduce the annual growth rate in our energy demand to less than 2 percent;

—to reduce gasoline consumption by 10 percent below its current level;

—to cut in half the portion of U.S. oil which is imported—from a potential level of 16 million barrels to 6 million barrels a day;

—to establish a strategic petroleum reserve of one billion barrels, more than a 6-month supply;

—to increase our coal production by about two-thirds to more than one billion tons a year;

—to insulate 90 percent of American homes and all new buildings;

—to use solar energy in more than 2½ million houses.

We will monitor our progress toward these goals year by year. Our plan will call for strict conservation measures if we fall behind. I can't tell you that these measures will be easy, nor will they be popular. But I think most of you realize that a policy which does not ask for changes or sacrifices would not be an effective policy at this late date.

This plan is essential to protect our jobs, our environment, our standard of living, and our future. Whether this plan truly makes a difference will not be decided now here in Washington but in every town and every factory, in every home and on every highway and every farm.

I believe that this can be a positive challenge. There is something especially American in the kinds of changes that we have to make. We've always been proud, through our history, of being efficient people. We've always been proud of our ingenuity, our skill at answering questions. Now we need efficiency and ingenuity more than ever.

We've always been proud of our leadership in the world. And now we have a chance again to give the world a positive example.

We've always been proud of our vision of the future. We've always wanted to give our children and our grandchildren a world richer in possibilities than we have had ourselves. They are the ones that we must provide for now. They are the ones who will suffer most if we don't act.

I've given you some of the principles of the plan. I'm sure that each of you will find something you don't like about the specifics of our proposal. It will demand that we make sacrifices and changes in every life. To some degree, the sacrifices will be painful—but so is any meaningful sacrifice. It will lead to some higher costs and to some greater inconvenience for everyone. But the sacrifices can be gradual, realistic, and they are necessary. Above all, they will be fair. No one will gain an unfair advantage through this plan. No one will be asked to bear an unfair burden.

We will monitor the accuracy of data from the oil and natural gas companies for the first time, so that we will always know their true production, supplies, reserves, and profits. Those citizens who insist on driving large, unnecessarily powerful cars must expect to pay more for that luxury.

We can be sure that all the special interest groups in the country will attack the part of this plan that affects them directly. They will say that sacrifice is fine as long as other people do it, but that their sacrifice is unreasonable or unfair or harmful to the country. If they succeed with this approach, then the burden on the ordinary citizen, who is not organized into an interest group, would be crushing.

There should be only one test for this program—whether it will help our country. Other generations of Americans have faced and mastered great challenges. I have faith that meeting this challenge will make our own lives even richer. If you will join me so that we can work together with patriotism and courage, we will again prove that our great Nation can lead the world into an age of peace, independence, and freedom.

Thank you very much, and good night.

2

DAVID STOCKMAN

The Wrong War? The Case
against a National Energy Policy

Fall 1978

*In 1978, Congressman David Stockman (R-Mich.) responded to Carter's
speech in an article published in a leading journal controlled by neo-
conservatives. Beginning in the late 1960s, this group of intellectuals
argued for American support of Israel, against affirmative action and
expansion of the welfare state, and for the efficient solution of social problems by market forces.*

When President Carter declared the energy crisis so serious for the
future political, economic and security interests of the nation that it
required a response amounting to the "moral equivalent of war," his
call to arms was met with nearly universal acclaim. To be sure, there
was much disagreement about the tactics of battle. But the twin tenets
of Carter's declaration—that the world was running out of energy and
that the U.S. faced grave peril unless it cured its "energy alcoholism"
and consequent dependence upon imported oil—became axiomatic in
all subsequent debate. . . .

One year later, the grand civilian mobilization proposed by the
Carter Administration to surmount this energy peril has not even been
launched. Congress has refused to approve even one of the heavy
artillery pieces requested by the Administration—the crude oil equal-
ization tax, a 50 cent tax on gasoline, industrial oil and gas consumption taxes, and a stiff forced-draft coal conversion program. . . .

. . . What we are experiencing just now may not be a political failure
at all, but rather a *remarkable political success.* Despite heavy odds, the
political system has not been panicked by momentary energy jingo-
ism. We have declined to launch what would have become a disas-
trous, inextricable engagement in an unnecessary war. It may be that

David Stockman, "The Wrong War? The Case against a National Energy Policy," *Public
Interest,* 53 (Fall 1978): 3–7, 10, 15, 16, 18–19, 21, 31, 37, 39–40, 44.

the true political task before us is not a renewed effort to mobilize our national resources for battle against energy shortages, oil imports, and related perils, but to confirm the implicit judgment of the electorate and mothball the motley energy army—such as it is—that we have erroneously called to arms. . . .

The underlying commitment to national energy autarky[1] rests on three axiomatic assumptions about the world energy condition. . . .

The first axiom is that the world faces the *imminent exhaustion of conventional fossil fuels* and that the "business-as-usual" workings of the marketplace are totally inadequate to respond to impending supply shortfalls. As the world's most powerful economy, the U.S. must therefore take the lead in politically managing the indicated transition to a low-energy, non-petroleum-based society. The second is that regardless of the precise state of potential world supplies or the timetable for depletion, *the world energy marketplace was irremediably impaired by the events of October 1973.* The market has been superseded by a politically motivated cartel presenting every manner of economic and national security peril to those nations which fail to take prudent steps toward insulating their economies from its reach. The final assumption is that *home grown energy is better,* and that by reducing imports through NEP-type[2] substitution and conservation schemes we will improve our balance of payments, strengthen the dollar, and enhance the performance of the domestic economy.

The first two propositions merit serious analysis and comprise the burden of that which follows. The third is a manifestation of economic wishful thinking, and can be refuted without much difficulty.

Hothouse Energy: A Dubious Bargain

At bottom, the notion that "home grown energy is better" implies a radical rejection of the global trading system and the law of comparative advantage[3] on which it is premised. . . .

. . . Any attempt to displace the 3 to 5 billion barrels per year in imported liquid and gaseous fuels that will likely be required late in the next decade would impose a cost-penalty on the economy in the range of $40 to $70 billion per year. The result would be a substantial, unnec-

---

[1]Autarky is a policy based on authoritarian power.

[2]"National energy plan" (NEP) was the term used to describe Carter's comprehensive policy.

[3]According to the law of comparative advantage, some nations can more efficiently produce certain commodities, such as oil.

essary loss in national output, and an artificially high domestic-energy-cost structure which would reduce the competitiveness of our exports and increase the cost-advantage of imports. . . .

The Myth of Imminent Depletion

If the case for energy autarky cannot rest on its intrinsic economic merits, it might nevertheless be made on the basis of postulated fundamental defects in the world market. Easiest to refute of these defenses of autarky is the assertion that conventional world supplies are nearing exhaustion.

Since the catalytic event which triggered the current march toward an autarky-based national energy policy occurred in the global context—the embargo crisis of October 1973—it did not take much of a leap in logic to assume that the U.S. oil and gas predicament was universal. After all, the cartel justified its action in the name of conservation and stretching dwindling oil supplies to cover the impending transition to the post-petroleum age.

The empirical data all point to the opposite conclusion, however. Even had it been known at the time of the embargo that the planet would refuse to give up one additional barrel of oil or gas reserves, there still would have remained a ready-to-produce worldwide inventory of proven reserves capable of sustaining consumption for more than a quarter-century. This hardly seems a basis for panic. . . .

Overall, the planet's accessible natural hydrocarbon reserves readily exceed 20 trillion barrels. *This is the equivalent of five centuries of consumption at current rates.* . . . The case for fossil-fuel exhaustion simply cannot rest on physical scarcity or the stinginess of the planet. Perforce it must assume a failure of man or his economic institutions.

Economic Events

One such failure is widely believed to have occurred in October 1973. Because OPEC sprang on the world sphinx-like out of the turmoil of the last Middle East war, it has been assumed that the original huge oil-price boosts were largely *political events,* reflecting the new-found political will, cooperation, and self-assertion of the Persian Gulf producers and their lesser oil-producing allies. Having successfully exerted political control over a substantial share of the world's crude oil reserve, so the argument goes, the cartel has essentially abolished any semblance of a normal world marketplace. If the laws of supply and demand have been revoked, and the predictability and reliability they generate are absent, neither the U.S. nor any other major industrial nation can afford to treat oil as just another commodity in world trade, the argument runs. Political usurpation of the market abroad must be countered with politically managed insulation of the market at home. . . .

There is a strong case to be made, however, that the October 1973 and subsequent price boosts were almost entirely *economic events;* that they were generated by nearly irresistible global economic forces; and that their timing originated as much in the domestic-energy production and consumption policies of the major industrial nations during the late 1960s and early 1970s as in the political turmoil of the Middle East and the emergence of an organized worldwide oil-producers' cartel.

The catalytic force in this process was delineation of the huge, ultra-low-cost Persian Gulf petroleum reserves during the 1950s, and their subsequent entry into the world energy-supply system. Once it was known that the Gulf contained several hundred billion barrels of reserves producible at less than 20 cents per barrel, the oil and other fuel-supply industries in the remainder of the world were destined for mothballs. The only potential escape from the withering competition of Persian Gulf oil was extra-market intervention—either in the form of home-market-protection policies or, ironically, through production of these resources under cartel or monopoly (high price) arrangements.

For two decades the world tried a little bit of both. Industries threatened by sudden changes in global comparative advantage do not die easily; instead, they seize the levers of political power and hang on for dear life behind protective barriers—quotas, tariffs, subsidies, "buy national" policies, and such other expedients as can be erected to compensate for lost economic advantage. . . .

The combination and timing of these developments was extraordinary. After 1970, nearly the entire increment of non-Communist world energy-demand growth had to be satisfied out of the Persian Gulf. . . .

The Consequences of OPEC: The Dark Side

. . . The dark side of the cartel comes into full relief. By effectively withholding part of the Persian Gulf hydrocarbon storehouse from the world economy, the cartel has temporarily denied the entire world the opportunity to prosper by tapping the prodigious amount of ready-to-use low-cost fuel reserves produced by the planet over the geologic ages. As it is, the planet's legacy in the Persian Gulf must now be supplanted by a quantum leap in the application of human and physical capital in order to unearth less easily obtainable resources from elsewhere on the globe.

This task can and is being accomplished. . . . But these additional supplies come only at a *huge cost in lost opportunities* for the world economy as a whole. The quantum leap in the resources required just to "run-in-place" in terms of energy supply means that less of other things can be produced, that output will be lower than otherwise, and that growth rates of worldwide physical production and economic well-being will be reduced. . . .

The Temporary Balance—and After

. . . Projections suggest that the global economy will prove itself sufficiently resilient to pacify the Persian Gulf cartel, but only at a substantial cost in terms of lower economic growth and reduced welfare for the people of the world. Yet there appears to be no alternative short of military intervention—a course fraught with even greater risk than that of reduced economic growth, given the relative parity of U.S./ Soviet military strength and the tenuous geopolitical balance that now prevails in the Middle East. . . .

The Necessity of Withdrawal

It is time to discard our medieval energy maps. There is no region filled with lurking dragons and other perils on the far side of the ocean. So rather than institute a politically imposed and bureaucratically managed and enforced regime of domestic-energy autarky, we need do little more than decontrol domestic energy prices, dismantle the energy bureaucracy, and allow the U.S. economy to equilibrate at the world level. Energy supply and demand will take care of itself, no less efficiently than were the commodity soybeans or Saran Wrap. And by thus encouraging full integration of the U.S. economy into the world marketplace's search for the least-cost-development sequence of our planet's prodigious remaining energy resources, we will produce the highest possible level of domestic economic growth and welfare.

Failure to do so will expose the American people to far greater dangers than any of the fictions emanating from our present energy bureaucrats. The most serious of these dangers is that we will squander massive amounts of economic resources on a continued futile and foolish quest for energy autarky. The economic pie will inevitably shrink as a result. And in the process we will saddle our economy and the American people with enormous amounts of political interference and bureaucratic management of their lives, so that the sphere of personal freedom will shrink as well. . . .

The only serious security threat is the prospect of Soviet intervention in the Gulf, either by direct military incursion or via client regimes. The fact is that the remaining oil and gas resources of the Persian Gulf have a present market value of some $16 trillion. The U.S. can no more afford to have these fall into Soviet hands than it can afford to lose Western Europe. The rate of current Persian Gulf production or the level of U.S. supply dependence makes absolutely no difference to the strategic importance of that region of the world. Were the U.S. to somehow achieve 100 percent energy independence, it would still have to counter overt Soviet aggression in the Persian Gulf with strategic power. To permit more than a trillion barrels of the planet's only remaining cheap-hydrocarbon resources to be annexed by the Soviet Union would pave the way for its speedy military and political domination of the world. Thus the *real* threat cannot be ameliorated with an NEP-type energy policy, or by former defense officials turned energy bureaucrats. The task of meeting that threat has belonged to the defense establishment all along.

3

TOM MORGANTHAU AND OTHERS

The Energy Plague

July 2, 1979

This news story tells of the dramatic events that Carter had to face when, on July 1, he returned from a trip during which he signed the SALT II treaty with the Soviet Union in Vienna (June 18) and met with leaders of the industrialized nations at a summit in Tokyo (June 29). During

Tom Morganthau, with John Walcott, Thomas M. DeFrank, Lea Donosky, and Holly Morris, "The Energy Plague," *Newsweek,* 2 July 1979, 22–24.

the summit, these leaders agreed on measures to cap their oil imports in order to pressure OPEC to reduce prices. Among the pictures accompanying the story were those of people lining up in their cars to get gas in New Jersey, truckers protesting in Wisconsin, cucumbers rotting in a warehouse because trucks could not pick them up to take them to markets, and guards protecting a refinery in Minnesota after strikers had prevented oil shipments.

Like some Biblical plague, the nation's energy problems just keep on multiplying. Truckers angry at the scarcity and high price of diesel fuel are in violent rebellion. Motorists searching for an open gas station must now contend with an odd-even rationing system that is spreading across the country. Office workers will soon find themselves sweating through a summer of 80-degree thermostat settings mandated by Washington. And for those stubborn souls who still insist that there is no energy crisis, the OPEC ministers will convene in Geneva this week and raise world oil prices by perhaps another $5 a barrel.

The nation's 100,000 independent, long-haul truckers pose the most immediate threat. Some of them simply pulled off the road in quiet rage last week. But a determined minority blockaded refineries and distribution centers with their eighteen-wheelers, and roving bands shot at the rigs of non-striking truckers in 23 states. So far, seven people have been injured and one killed. Produce began to rot in dozens of warehouses, mostly in the South and West, and meatpackers appealed to the President for Federal protection for their stalled shipments. Civil emergencies were declared in several states, and the National Guard was called out in Minnesota, Florida and at least seven other states. Jimmy Carter followed his dedication of solar-heating panels on the White House roof to invoke a grim warning. "Murder, vandalism and physical intimidation are criminal acts," he said, "and they will be treated as such."

As June gasoline allocations evaporated in a haze of summer driving and the psychology of scarcity took hold, odd-even rationing was imposed outside California for the first time since 1974. New York and Connecticut went first, followed by New Jersey, Maryland, Virginia and the District of Columbia. In oil-rich Texas, Gov. William Clements announced that odd-even rules will go into effect around Dallas, Ft. Worth and Houston this week—in the very shadow of the nation's biggest refineries. "Making Texans stand in line for gas is like making

Kansans stand in line for wheat," huffed the president of the state AFL-CIO, Harry Hubbard.

"Getting Ugly"

In southern Florida, Dade County officials ordered rationing to quell a gas panic triggered when truckers halted gasoline deliveries, and authorities in other states ordered limits on tank topping. The results were mixed: lines were shorter in some areas, unabated in others—but almost everywhere the gasoline crunch turned frayed nerves into deep worry and anger. "This country," said a White House staffer, "is getting ugly."

The worst news was yet to come: a new price boost from this week's OPEC meeting in Geneva. The best hope within the Carter Administration was that the official price would plateau around $20 a barrel, up from $14.55; at that level, optimists said, OPEC would only ratify the panoply of surcharges most of its members already collect. But analysts said the more significant issue at Geneva was whether the cartel would increase crude-oil production—and on that score, U.S. hopes were crushed last week. "The Saudi Government," Saudi Arabia's Crown Prince Fahd declared in an interview, "has not decided so far to increase production beyond the present 8.5 million barrels" per day. That left Carter heading for the Tokyo economic summit with only faint hopes of attaining consensus for action among the oil-consuming nations.

The barrage of bleak tidings could hardly have come at a worse time for Jimmy Carter. Just back from signing the strategic arms limitation treaty with the Soviet Union, Carter delivered one of the better speeches of his Presidency, a 40-minute televised address to Congress on SALT. But it was lost on the American public. A White House summary of telephone calls after the speech logged 113 messages on SALT and 382 on energy. Quite obviously, Carter will get little bounce from SALT in the public-opinion polls. The latest reading from Gallup last week showed Carter down to an approval rating of 29 per cent—a 17-point plunge in less than three months. "All the summits in the world aren't going to make Jimmy Carter popular," muttered a domestic adviser. "People want gas and they want lower prices."

Synthetics

But the wave of public anxiety over the metastasizing energy crisis at last has reached Capitol Hill—and Administration officials only recently sulking over the defeat of Carter's stand-by gas-rationing plan moved to capitalize on the new mood of urgency. Carter met with Congressional leaders to praise the "friendly competition between the Senate and the House and the executive branch" to promote production of synthetic fuels, and White House staffers prepared phase two of his energy plan for a mid-July debut. Its contents, as contemplated by a vast energy task force, will be subsidies to help the poor pay rising energy bills, more money for mass transit and probably a program to make synthetic oil from coal and oil shale. "You can say that the activity in Congress has driven us to a more concerted push toward energy independence," one Carterite said.

Moving to the quickened tempo, the House Ways and Means Committee voted to increase Carter's windfall-profits tax from $21.8 billion to $28.5 billion—and House Democrats began looking for ways to spend the proceeds on new energy sources. There was little doubt that the House would approve a bill to underwrite a major synthetic fuel program, and the prospects were bright for the solar-energy fund proposed by Carter at midweek. He declared that the U.S. could get 20 per cent of its energy from the sun by the year 2000, but the estimate included such renewable sources as hydroelectricity and wood. Majority Leader James Wright privately suggested a new pipeline to pump Alaskan crude from the Pacific coast to the upper Midwest— and there was talk of reviving, in some form, Carter's much-lamented stand-by gas-rationing plan.

Temperatures Rising

Carter also is ready to impose new Federal restrictions on thermostat settings in virtually every office, factory, store and restaurant in the nation—approximately 5 million buildings in all. Now being drafted by the Department of Energy, the rules will require that thermostats be set no lower than 80 degrees for summer cooling and no higher than 65 degrees for heating in winter. They are expected to take effect in early or mid-July—and the energy savings could reach 390,000 barrels of oil a day, about 2 per cent of U.S. consumption. The plan already is in effect in Federal offices nationwide, and tempers are rising with the temperature. In New Orleans last week, a group of Federal judges termed the edict "arbitrary, capricious and unreasonable" and, using the full weight of their judicial authority, ordered their thermostat lowered to 74.

The truckers' protest had much the same basis: a stubborn refusal to accept the Carter Administration's allocation of sacrifice. They want a 10 per cent freight surcharge rate to help compensate for higher fuel prices, but so far the government has offered only 6 per cent. They also object to a Department of Energy rule that gave diesel-fuel priority to farmers during spring planting—diverting already scarce fuel away from truck stops and driving up prices. As more and more independents stopped trucking, shipments of fresh produce and meat came nearly to a standstill. "When the President and all them senators can't get no steaks," drawled one Alabama driver last week, "then they'll do something."

"Full Force"

Other protesters used tougher tactics. Alabama trucker Robert Tate, 31, bled to death along state highway 72 after a sniper's bullet severed an artery in his knee; his was the first fatality of the increasingly violent strike. In the aftermath of the shooting, Gov. Fob James ordered armed escorts for convoys through his state and urged other truckers to arm themselves. "If someone shoots at you, threatens you, then you can use full force against them," James advised.

Police in Missoula, Mont., monitored death threats that were broadcast against non-strikers over citizens band radios, and a driver in Tennessee was wounded after heeding a CB call to stop his truck. "I saw the President on TV the other night," said grower J. D. Lowe III of Falfurrias, Texas. "All he could mention was the SALT II agreement. That doesn't do a damned bit of good for us—we've got a national emergency out here in the country. People are getting killed in the streets."

"Best Medicine"

The upsurge of violence prompted authorities in several states to protect truckers with armed escorts, and Carter volunteered the FBI to aid investigations of strike-related crimes. But Federal officials also moved to meet the strikers' demands. They repealed the rule that gave farmers priority for diesel fuel, and urged states to raise weight limits on trailer loads. And Carter got Sen. Edward Kennedy's support in formally proposing the wholesale deregulation of the trucking industry—a reform that could substantially benefit independent truckers by allowing them to haul freight now carried only by the licensed trucking companies. "The best anti-inflation medicine is real competition," Carter said. "According to the Council on Wage and Price Stability, this trucking deregulation bill will save American consumers $5 billion."

The truckers' action also aggravated the gasoline shortage. In Wisconsin, Minnesota and Rhode Island, strikers blockaded gasoline deliveries, causing acute spot shortages until authorities forced them to stop. In south Florida, the National Guard was ordered to make deliveries to the area's bone-dry stations. The scent of gas triggered a Pavlovian[1] response from motorists: when civilian driver Al Jones wheeled a rare load of gas to a suburban Miami station, 25 cars instinctively followed him to the pumps. "I felt like the Pied Piper," Jones said as the crowd cheered.

"Worst Ever"

Predictably, rationing got off to a bumpy start where the shortages were worst. Panicky motorists bluffed and bribed to beat the odd-even system, and station operators took most of the heat. "One guy I didn't serve because his tank was almost full said he'd come back and drop a hand grenade on me," said Frank Mastrobuoni, a New Jersey station attendant. "There is panic at the pumps," said Mac Victor of the New York State Association of Service Stations. "It's the worst it's ever been."

The brutal competition for fuel pitted motorist against motorist, trucker against farmer, region against region—a sobering illustration of the zero-sum conflicts inherent in the intensifying energy crunch. In California, where odd-even rationing is now a way of life, the reaction to the East's belated scramble was smug—and frazzled New Yorkers, paying up to $1.50 a gallon after hours in line, were irate. "I want the energy people in Washington to tell us where the gas is, and to use the special Federal authority to prevent price gouging and hoarding," said Gov. Hugh Carey.

Federal officials continued to insist the crisis would ease slightly in the months ahead—but there was little doubt that as Americans competed for scarce fuel supplies, the summer of '79 would be a scorcher.

---

[1]Ivan Pavlov (1849–1936) was a Russian psychologist who proved that animals respond automatically to stimuli.

4

NATIONAL REVIEW

Carter on the Titanic: *Editorial*

July 27, 1979

Written while Carter was still at the domestic summit at Camp David but published shortly after his July 15 speech, this editorial appeared in the nation's leading conservative magazine. It makes clear the nature of opposition to Carter from the political right and explores the increasingly difficult situation the president faced within the Democratic party.

Gasoline is President Carter's Vietnam—important enough in itself, but more so in the way it strips bare his political vulnerability.

Carter no doubt has his personal shortcomings—his ineloquence, his rationalist apolitical mentality, his self-righteousness, his tropism for third-rate personnel, his provincial naïveté in foreign policy. At that level, Woodrow Wilson time is with us again. But fundamentally Carter's problems have always been political, and have to do with the deep and unbridgeable splits within the Democratic Party. Each of Carter's energy options can only exacerbate those splits.

The Left Democrats want gas rationing, wage and price controls, severe and imposed conservation measures, heavy taxation, and the extension of government controls. Moderate Democrats want deregulation and market pricing, which they see as increasing supplies and undercutting OPEC. There's no way to reconcile that division.

Again, Carter has had training as a nuclear engineer. He gives every indication of understanding that the U.S. must press forward with nuclear power. Can he say so? Can he, as part of his energy speech, demand that hobbling restrictions on nuclear development be struck down? If he does that, he risks the support of the growing antinuclear constituency—and Governor Moonbeam,[1] out in Sacramento, is preparing to run on that issue.

---

[1]California governor Jerry Brown, who critics felt was too influenced by the counterculture of the 1960s.

"Carter on the *Titanic*," *National Review*, 27 July 1979, B105.

The U.S. has a five-hundred-year supply of coal. Mining it, processing it into synthetic fuels, and burning it will offend the environmentalists, who have a lot of clout on the Democratic Left. We could save millions of gallons of gasoline by relaxing some of our myriad pollution regulations, but Ralph Nader would not sit still for that. Unleaded gasoline was imposed on us on environmental grounds. It is inefficient.

These issues divide Democrats, but they also represent social-class issues. They divide haves and have-nots. The affluent want clean air, tourist-free forests, uncrowded and oil-free beaches, happy caribou and snail-darters. The non-affluent want jobs, raises, economic expansion, and enough gas to get the family to a public beach.

During the 1976 primaries, Carter proved himself to be a virtuoso at papering over these contradictions. Once in office, however, he was crippled by them all across the board.

The style in which Carter canceled his energy speech reflected both petulance and panic. Nor did his third-rate staff make any attempt to save him from embarrassment. Even a first-rate staff, however, would find it difficult to come up with a speech that would satisfy Carter's divided constituency.

Carter has withdrawn, like Moses to the Mountain, gathering about him various tribal representatives. He hopes to descend, delivering the Word of the Lord.

But he does not possess that Word, because of his divided constituency.

From a political perspective, that is the meaning of the Kennedy furor. For a Democrat, to be for Kennedy in 1980 is a convenient way of not making any hard choices in 1979.

2

Religion, Materialism, and Leadership:
Traditions on Which Carter Drew

In the spring of 1979, as the second wave of the energy crisis grew in intensity, political pollster Patrick Caddell succeeded in convincing Carter to read the works of authors who focused on the connections between affluence, leadership, and religion. As Carter considered how he might respond to the energy crisis of 1979, Caddell persuaded the president to educate Americans on the moral and spiritual dimensions of what the nation faced. Carter's intellectual engagement was both impressive and politically perilous. Most people faced with rapidly increasing prices and dramatically decreasing supplies of energy wanted abundant energy at reasonable prices rather than an education informed by what leading thinkers had to teach them—especially if that teaching involved accusations of how materialistic and self-indulgent they were.

Caddell's advice came through forcefully in his April 23, 1979, memo titled "Of Crisis and Opportunity" (discussed in part one). In his memo, Caddell tried to strengthen the president's conviction that the problems he and the nation faced were not merely political and practical but spiritual and philosophical as well. In doing so, Caddell intensified a battle in the White House over the approach Carter would use in addressing the energy crisis. The documents in this chapter are among the sources the president read. The writings of Alexis de Tocqueville, Daniel Bell, Christopher Lasch, and Robert Bellah reinforced core elements of Carter's beliefs that were grounded in his long-standing Baptist faith. What Carter read in the spring and early summer of 1979 buttressed his convictions that affluence had made Americans self-indulgent, that the pursuit of materialism had eroded people's commitment to the public good, that religion would help restrain people's greed, and that moral leadership would place the nation on a more righteous path.

The French aristocrat Alexis de Tocqueville (1805–1859) visited the United States in 1831–32. When he returned to France, he wrote *Democracy in America,* first translated into English in 1835 and 1840. Ever since, his book has remained a penetrating and influential interpretation of American life. Popular in the 1950s when anti-Communists relied on it as a counter to those who admired the Soviet Union, *Democracy in America* attracted renewed interest in the 1970s from intellectuals and the president. In the selections reprinted here, Tocqueville explored Americans' love of affluence, its impact on public life, and how religion and leadership might counteract its deleterious effects. Carter's engagement with what Tocqueville wrote almost a century and a half earlier only strengthened his view of American society.

Carter also read the writings of one of the nation's leading sociologists, Harvard professor Daniel Bell. Born in 1919, Bell grew up in New York in an impoverished, Jewish immigrant household. He was one of the most influential American public intellectuals of his generation. Carter read Bell's book *The Cultural Contradictions of Capitalism* (1976), which offered a sweeping and complex analysis of America, including that the excessive pursuit of affluence and self-gratification threatened to tear it apart. His tone was pessimistic, almost apocalyptic. The title of Bell's book referred to three realms that in an earlier age he believed had operated in harmony but were now in tension with one another. The first was the "techno-economic," ruled by rationality, efficiency, and economizing. The second was the political arena, in which expanding claims for social justice and equality had led to an ever greater sense of entitlement among citizens. The third was the culture, increasingly governed by the quest for self-fulfillment. The ascendancy of the cultural realm in contemporary America, with its emphasis on individualistic expressiveness, had eroded the commitment to hard work and the public good. The conflicts between an economy based on rationality and efficiency, a political order based on equality and justice, and a culture based on pleasure had, Bell thought, brought the nation to a breaking point.

Bell offered two solutions to the dire situation he diagnosed. With secular meanings proving illusory, modernism and cultural radicalism exhausted, and bourgeois values devastated, religion might make culture more moral, restore the connections between generations, and encourage people to focus less on self-fulfillment. In addition, Bell called for the restoration of a commitment to a public good that transcended individual desires. He centered his hopes on what he called a public household, something that was market oriented but nonetheless did not abandon larger social goals. The sense of a common good would foster civic responsibility that would prompt people to turn away from private pleasures.

Carter invited Bell to the White House for dinner and an evening of conversation on May 30, 1979. During dinner, the president turned to Bell, who was sitting on his immediate left, and began an intense conversation that lasted about twenty minutes. After mentioning that he had read *The Cultural Contradictions of Capitalism,* Carter asked Bell whether he thought Americans would return to religion. Bell responded by discussing how religion might provide citizens with a greater sense of continuity with the past. Bell also emphasized how critical to people's self-respect and social decency was a reasonable standard of living, the provision of which was the basic responsibility of the community. He contrasted this with the satisfaction of wants, which were more psychological in nature. The president was most interested in the distinction between needs and wants.* As Carter's own handwritten notes indicate, Carter understood the central arguments of Bell's book.

Also at that dinner was Christopher Lasch (1932–1994), whose *Culture of Narcissism: American Life in an Age of Diminishing Expectations* had appeared in early 1979. After growing up in the Midwest, Lasch, like Bell, had shifted over the course of his life from an embrace of radicalism to what he considered a sympathetic reconsideration of its lessons. A professor at the University of Rochester, Lasch was one of the nation's most widely read historians turned public intellectuals. In *The Culture of Narcissism,* Lasch articulated a tragic vision of American life in which his analysis of affluence, history, and self-fulfillment played a central role. He argued that the material well-being that liberal individualists and corporate capitalists alike celebrated had trapped people, rather than liberating them, by stripping them of sources of genuine satisfaction. The search for self-fulfillment through consumption and therapy, he asserted, had turned America into a hedonist society. All these forces undermined real work, an authentic sense of self, and a morally grounded faith.

During the spring of 1979 and at Camp David in early July, White House staff members gave visitors copies of Lasch's *Culture of Nar-*

---

*Daniel Bell, "Dinner at the White House," 1 Sept. 1979, Memoir: Dinner at the White House, Daniel Bell: Writings, September 1979, Daniel Bell Papers, Cambridge, Mass. (hereafter cited as DBP), 22–25, 27.

cissism. The book appealed to the president and some members of his staff because of Lasch's insistence that Americans were increasingly narcissistic, excessively tempted by what the author and the president saw as the way Americans indulged themselves by consuming excessively.

Carter also read Robert Bellah's article "Human Conditions for a Good Society," to which Caddell had called his attention. Born in 1927 and growing up in Los Angeles in a Presbyterian household, Bellah had been radicalized in the 1940s. In 1979, he was a practicing Episcopalian, a professor of sociology at the University of California at Berkeley, and the nation's leading sociologist of religion. In his writings of the 1970s, he spelled out complicated arguments in which religion, socialism, and citizenship served as counters to self-interest and affluence. His views emerged most fully in *The Broken Covenant: American Civil Religion in Time of Trial* (1975). When Carter began to write the speech he delivered on July 15, 1979, he recalled Bellah's article, which offered a condensed version of *The Broken Covenant.* Bellah contrasted the biblical tradition, which emphasized a covenant that transcended self-interest and involved concern for others, with industrial capitalism and the pursuit of luxuries. His own preference was for a reawakening of spirituality and a decentralized society and economy, which he hoped would undergird a revitalized and morally based public life.

Carter invited Bellah to the domestic summit at Camp David on July 10, 1979. What appealed to Carter was Bellah's contrast between an individualism based on market orientation and a commitment to a communal, public good grounded in historic and religious traditions. In anticipation of the visit, Bellah noted the opposing parts of Carter's outlook, how his individual morality, derived from a Baptist tradition in which there was little sense of responsibility for the public realm, conflicted with his technocratic mentality. He worried that fierce struggles among social groups might emerge if the nation continued to face battles over shrinking resources. He had doubts that a culture of narcissism gripped America, for he saw, even in California, opposing traditions of public concern. Consequently, he wanted Carter to reinvigorate the nation's sense of its public commitments and to do so by relying on moral and religious traditions rather than technocratic imperatives.*

---

*Robert N. Bellah, Handwritten Notes, probably 9 July 1979, Robert N. Bellah Papers, Berkeley, Calif.

5

ALEXIS DE TOCQUEVILLE

Democracy in America

1835 and 1840

In the spring of 1979, as Carter tried to understand what ailed America, he read sections such as these that Tocqueville had written after he visited the United States in 1831–32. The Frenchman's analysis resonated with the president's conviction that what America faced was a moral and spiritual crisis born of the nation's excessive love of material comforts that religion and moral leadership would counter.

CHAPTER X

Of the Taste for Physical Well-Being in America

... When [in a democratic society] the distinctions of ranks are obliterated and privileges are destroyed, when hereditary property is subdivided and education and freedom are widely diffused, the desire of acquiring the comforts of the world haunts the imagination of the poor, and the dread of losing them that of the rich. Many scanty fortunes spring up; those who possess them have a sufficient share of physical gratifications to conceive a taste for these pleasures, not enough to satisfy it. They never procure them without exertion, and they never indulge in them without apprehension. They are therefore always straining to pursue or to retain gratifications so delightful, so imperfect, so fugitive.

... The passion for physical comforts is essentially a passion of the middle classes; with those classes it grows and spreads, with them it is preponderant. From them it mounts into the higher orders of society and descends into the mass of the people. ...

Alexis de Tocqueville, *Democracy in America*, trans. Henry Reeve (1835 and 1840; repr., New York: Knopf, 1945), 2:129–33, 140–45, 147, 150.

. . . The love of well-being has now become the predominant taste of the nation; the great current of human passions runs in that channel and sweeps everything along in its course.

CHAPTER XI

Peculiar Effects of the Love of Physical Gratifications in Democratic Times

. . . The taste for physical gratifications leads a democratic people into no such excesses [as was true in an aristocratic society]. The love of well-being is there displayed as a tenacious, exclusive, universal passion, but its range is confined. To build enormous palaces, to conquer or to mimic nature, to ransack the world in order to gratify the passions of a man, is not thought of, but to add a few yards of land to your field, to plant an orchard, to enlarge a dwelling, to be always making life more comfortable and convenient, to avoid trouble, and to satisfy the smallest wants without effort and almost without cost. These are small objects, but the soul clings to them; it dwells upon them closely and day by day, till they at last shut out the rest of the world and sometimes intervene between itself and heaven. . . .

The special taste that the men of democratic times entertain for physical enjoyments is not naturally opposed to the principles of public order; nay, it often stands in need of order that it may be gratified. Nor is it adverse to regularity of morals, for good morals contribute to public tranquillity and are favorable to industry. It may even be frequently combined with a species of religious morality; men wish to be as well off as they can in this world without forgoing their chance of another. Some physical gratifications cannot be indulged in without crime; from such they strictly abstain. The enjoyment of others is sanctioned by religion and morality; to these the heart, the imagination, and life itself are unreservedly given up, till, in snatching at these lesser gifts, men lose sight of those more precious possessions which constitute the glory and the greatness of mankind.

The reproach I address to the principle of equality is not that it leads men away in the pursuit of forbidden enjoyments, but that it absorbs them wholly in quest of those which are allowed. By these means a kind of virtuous materialism may ultimately be established in the world, which would not corrupt, but enervate, the soul and noiselessly unbend its springs of action.

CHAPTER XIV

How the Taste for Physical Gratification Is United in America to Love of Freedom and Attention to Public Affairs

... There is, indeed, a most dangerous passage in the history of a democratic people. When the taste for physical gratifications among them has grown more rapidly than their education and their experience of free institutions, the time will come when men are carried away and lose all self-restraint at the sight of the new possessions they are about to obtain. In their intense and exclusive anxiety to make a fortune they lose sight of the close connection that exists between the private fortune of each and the prosperity of all. It is not necessary to do violence to such a people in order to strip them of the rights they enjoy; they themselves willingly loosen their hold. The discharge of political duties appears to them to be a troublesome impediment which diverts them from their occupations and business. . . .

... The Americans believe their freedom to be the best instrument and surest safeguard of their welfare; they are attached to the one by the other. They by no means think that they are not called upon to take a part in public affairs; they believe, on the contrary, that their chief business is to secure for themselves a government which will allow them to acquire the things they covet and which will not debar them from the peaceful enjoyment of those possessions which they have already acquired.

CHAPTER XV

How Religious Belief Sometimes Turns the Thoughts of Americans to Immaterial Pleasures

... I have endeavored to point out, in another part of this work, the causes to which the maintenance of the political institutions of the Americans is attributable, and religion appeared to be one of the most prominent among them. I am now treating of the Americans in an individual capacity, and I again observe that religion is not less useful to each citizen than to the whole state. The Americans show by their practice that they feel the high necessity of imparting morality to democratic communities by means of religion. What they think of themselves in this respect is a truth of which every democratic nation ought to be thoroughly persuaded. . . .

But while man takes delight in this honest and lawful pursuit of his own well-being [through education and freedom], it is to be apprehended that in the end he may lose the use of his sublimest faculties, and that while he is busied in improving all around him, he may at length degrade himself. Here, and here only, does the peril lie. It should therefore be the unceasing object of the legislators of democracies and of all the virtuous and enlightened men who live there to raise the souls of their fellow citizens and keep them lifted up towards heaven. It is necessary that all who feel an interest in the future destinies of democratic society should unite, and that all should make joint and continual efforts to diffuse the love of the infinite, lofty aspirations, and a love of pleasures not of earth. . . .

Materialism, among all nations, is a dangerous disease of the human mind; but it is more especially to be dreaded among a democratic people because it readily amalgamates with that vice which is most familiar to the heart under such circumstances. Democracy encourages a taste for physical gratification; this taste, if it become excessive, soon disposes men to believe that all is matter only; and materialism, in its turn, hurries them on with mad impatience to these same delights; such is the fatal circle within which democratic nations are driven round. It were well that they should see the danger and hold back.

Most religions are only general, simple, and practical means of teaching men the doctrine of the immortality of the soul. That is the greatest benefit which a democratic people derives from its belief, and hence belief is more necessary to such a people than to all others. . . .

What means then remain in the hands of constituted authorities to bring men back to spiritual opinions or to hold them fast to the religion by which those opinions are suggested?

My answer will do me harm in the eyes of politicians. I believe that the sole effectual means which governments can employ in order to have the doctrine of the immortality of the soul duly respected is always to act as if they believed in it themselves; and I think that it is only by scrupulous conformity to religious morality in great affairs that they can hope to teach the community at large to know, to love, and to observe it in the lesser concerns of life. . . .

CHAPTER XVII

How, When Conditions Are Equal and Skepticism Is Rife, It Is Important to Direct Human Actions to Distant Objects

... When everyone is constantly striving to change his position, when an immense field for competition is thrown open to all, when wealth is amassed or dissipated in the shortest possible space of time amid the turmoil of democracy, visions of sudden and easy fortunes, of great possessions easily won and lost, of chance under all its forms haunt the mind. The instability of society itself fosters the natural instability of man's desires. In the midst of these perpetual fluctuations of his lot, the present looms large upon his mind; it hides the future, which becomes indistinct, and men seek only to think about tomorrow.

In those countries in which, unhappily, irreligion and democracy coexist, philosophers and those in power ought to be always striving to place the objects of human actions far beyond man's immediate range. Adapting himself to the spirit of his country and his age, the moralist must learn to vindicate his principles in that position. He must constantly endeavor to show his contemporaries that even in the midst of the perpetual commotion around them it is easier than they think to conceive and to execute protracted undertakings. He must teach them that although the aspect of mankind may have changed, the methods by which men may provide for their prosperity in this world are still the same; and that among democratic nations as well as elsewhere it is only by resisting a thousand petty selfish passions of the hour that the general and unquenchable passion for happiness can be satisfied.

The task of those in power is not less clearly marked out. At all times it is important that those who govern nations should act with a view to the future: but this is even more necessary in democratic and skeptical ages than in any others. By acting thus the leading men of democracies not only make public affairs prosperous, but also teach private individuals, by their example, the art of managing their private concerns. . . .

6

JIMMY CARTER

Handwritten Notes on Conversation with Daniel Bell at the White House

May 30, 1979

After dinner at the White House on May 30, 1979, at which Harvard sociologist Daniel Bell sat next to the president, Carter retired to his private quarters, where he listed the guests and summarized Bell's ideas. In many ways, what Bell argued dovetailed with what Tocqueville had written and with Carter's own sense of the spiritual dimensions of the crisis Americans faced.

Bill Moyers[1]
Charles Peters = Wash[ington] Monthly
Haynes Johnson = W[ashington] Post
Jesse Jackson
Christopher Lasch, Culture of Narcissism
Daniel Bell Cult[ural] Contradictions of Capitalism
John Gardner
Pat Cadell [*sic*]

Bell
Limits of mundane → religion
Power → political order
Econ[omy] = effic   Polity = Equal[ity]   Cult[ure] = Self-realization
Self gratification
Present—not past nor future

---

[1]In 1979, Bill Moyers was a senior news analyst for CBS; Charles Peters was editor of *Washington Monthly*, an influential neoliberal publication; Haynes Johnson was a columnist for the *Washington Post;* Jesse Jackson was head of Operation PUSH, a civil rights organization; John W. Gardner, author of *Morale* (1978), had just completed a stint as founder and chair of Common Cause, a citizen lobbyist group.

Jimmy Carter, Handwritten Notes on Conversation with Daniel Bell at the White House, 30 May 1979, Office of Staff Secretary: Presidential Handwriting File, box 133, folder "5/30/79," Jimmy Carter Presidential Library, Atlanta, Ga. (hereafter cited as JCPL).

5/30/79

Bill Moyers
Charles Peters = Wash monthly
Haynes Johnson - W Post
Jesse Jackson
Christopher Lasch, Culture & Narcissism
Daniel Bell — Cult. Contradiction of
Cap talism
John Gardner
Pat Cadell

ref

Limits of mundane → religion
Power → political order
Econ = effic. Polity. equal. Cult: self
respect
Self gratification
Present - not past nor future
Losing confidence in future
Traditional values ↗
Era of limits vs demands ↗
Crisis in culture, then politics?
Productivity → work ethic
Role of govt + or - ?
Can families be strengthened?
How to make tangibles intangible.
Presidential leadership
Can America be rejuvenated?

Jimmy Carter's handwritten notes on conversation with Daniel Bell at the White House, May 30, 1979.

Losing confidence in future
Traditional values ⤳
Era of limits vs demands ↗
Crisis in culture, then politics?
Productivity ↓ work ethic
Role of gov't + or – ?
Can families be strengthened?
How to mix tangible w/ intangible.
Presidential leadership
Can America be rejuvenated?

7

CHRISTOPHER LASCH

The Culture of Narcissism

1979

Christopher Lasch offered a provocative analysis of Americans as increasingly narcissistic, tempted by what the author and the president saw as excessive consumption. Lasch's message coincided with the president's sense of a nation in the midst of a spiritual crisis born of a value-destroying materialism, disconnection from the past, pessimism about the future, and distrust of American institutions.

Hardly more than a quarter-century after Henry Luce proclaimed "the American century," American confidence has fallen to a low ebb. Those who recently dreamed of world power now despair of governing the city of New York.[1] Defeat in Vietnam, economic stagnation, and the impending exhaustion of natural resources have produced a

---

[1] In 1941, Henry Luce (1898–1967), one of the founders of *Time* and *Life* magazines, declared the twentieth century "the American Century." Lasch was contrasting that sense of confidence with the concern in the late 1970s that New York City was ungovernable.

Christopher Lasch, *The Culture of Narcissism: American Life in an Age of Diminishing Expectations* (New York: Norton, 1979), xiii–xviii.

mood of pessimism in higher circles, which spreads through the rest of society as people lose faith in their leaders. The same crisis of confidence grips other capitalist countries as well. In Europe, the growing strength of communist parties, the revival of fascist movements, and a wave of terrorism all testify, in different ways, to the weakness of established régimes and to the exhaustion of established tradition. Even Canada, long a bastion of stolid bourgeois dependability, now faces in the separatist movement in Quebec a threat to its very existence as a nation.

The international dimensions of the current malaise indicate that it cannot be attributed to an American failure of nerve. Bourgeois society seems everywhere to have used up its store of constructive ideas. It has lost both the capacity and the will to confront the difficulties that threaten to overwhelm it. The political crisis of capitalism reflects a general crisis of western culture, which reveals itself in a pervasive despair of understanding the course of modern history or of subjecting it to rational direction. Liberalism, the political theory of the ascendant bourgeoisie, long ago lost the capacity to explain events in the world of the welfare state and the multinational corporation; nothing has taken its place. Politically bankrupt, liberalism is intellectually bankrupt as well. The sciences it has fostered, once confident of their ability to dispel the darkness of the ages, no longer provide satisfactory explanations of the phenomena they profess to elucidate. Neoclassical economic theory cannot explain the coexistence of unemployment and inflation; sociology retreats from the attempt to outline a general theory of modern society; academic psychology retreats from the challenge of Freud into the measurement of trivia. The natural sciences, having made exaggerated claims for themselves, now hasten to announce that science offers no miracle cures for social problems.

In the humanities, demoralization has reached the point of a general admission that humanistic study has nothing to contribute to an understanding of the modern world. Philosophers no longer explain the nature of things or pretend to tell us how to live. Students of literature treat the text not as a representation of the real world but as a reflection of the artist's inner state of mind. Historians admit to a "sense of the irrelevance of history," in David Donald's[2] words, "and of the bleakness of the new era we are entering." Because liberal culture has always depended so heavily on the study of history, the collapse of

---

[2] A Civil War historian.

that culture finds an especially poignant illustration in the collapse of the historical faith, which formerly surrounded the record of public events with an aura of moral dignity, patriotism, and political optimism. Historians in the past assumed that men learned from their previous mistakes. Now that the future appears troubled and uncertain, the past appears "irrelevant" even to those who devote their lives to investigating it. "The age of abundance has ended," Donald writes. "The 'lessons' taught by the American past are today not merely irrelevant but dangerous. . . . Perhaps my most useful function would be to disenthrall [students] from the spell of history, to help them see the irrelevance of the past, . . . [to] remind them to what a limited extent humans control their own destiny."

Such is the view from the top—the despairing view of the future now widely shared by those who govern society, shape public opinion, and supervise the scientific knowledge on which society depends. If on the other hand we ask what the common man thinks about his prospects, we find plenty of evidence to confirm the impression that the modern world faces the future without hope, but we also find another side of the picture, which qualifies that impression and suggests that western civilization may yet generate the moral resources to transcend its present crisis. A pervasive distrust of those in power has made society increasingly difficult to govern, as the governing class repeatedly complains without understanding its own contribution to the difficulty; but this same distrust may furnish the basis of a new capacity for self-government, which would end by doing away with the need that gives rise to a governing class in the first place. What looks to political scientists like voter apathy may represent a healthy skepticism about a political system in which public lying has become endemic and routine. A distrust of experts may help to diminish the dependence on experts that has crippled the capacity for self-help.

Modern bureaucracy has undermined earlier traditions of local action, the revival and extension of which holds out the only hope that a decent society will emerge from the wreckage of capitalism. The inadequacy of solutions dictated from above now forces people to invent solutions from below. Disenchantment with governmental bureaucracies has begun to extend to corporate bureaucracies as well—the real centers of power in contemporary society. In small towns and crowded urban neighborhoods, even in suburbs, men and women have initiated modest experiments in cooperation, designed to defend their rights against the corporations and the state. The "flight from politics," as it appears to the managerial and political elite, may signify the citizen's growing unwillingness to take part in the political system as a consumer of prefabricated spectacles. It may signify, in other words, not a retreat from politics at all but the beginnings of a general political revolt.

Much could be written about the signs of new life in the United States. This book, however, describes a way of life that is dying—the culture of competitive individualism, which in its decadence has carried the logic of individualism to the extreme of a war of all against all, the pursuit of happiness to the dead end of a narcissistic preoccupation with the self. Strategies of narcissistic survival now present themselves as emancipation from the repressive conditions of the past, thus giving rise to a "cultural revolution" that reproduces the worst features of the collapsing civilization it claims to criticize. Cultural radicalism has become so fashionable, and so pernicious in the support it unwittingly provides for the status quo, that any criticism of contemporary society that hopes to get beneath the surface has to criticize, at the same time, much of what currently goes under the name of radicalism.

Events have rendered liberationist critiques of modern society hopelessly out of date—and much of an earlier Marxist critique as well. Many radicals still direct their indignation against the authoritarian family, repressive sexual morality, literary censorship, the work ethic, and other foundations of bourgeois order that have been weakened or destroyed by advanced capitalism itself. These radicals do not see that the "authoritarian personality" no longer represents the prototype of the economic man. Economic man himself has given way to the psychological man of our times—the final product of bourgeois individualism. The new narcissist is haunted not by guilt but by anxiety. He seeks not to inflict his own certainties on others but to find a meaning in life. Liberated from the superstitions of the past, he doubts even the reality of his own existence. Superficially relaxed and tolerant, he finds little use for dogmas of racial and ethnic purity but at the same time forfeits the security of group loyalties and regards everyone as a rival for the favors conferred by a paternalistic state. His sexual attitudes are permissive rather than puritanical, even though his emancipation from ancient taboos brings him no sexual peace. Fiercely competitive in his demand for approval and acclaim, he distrusts competition because he associates it unconsciously with an unbridled urge to destroy. Hence he repudiates the competitive ideologies that flourished at an earlier stage of capitalist development and distrusts even their limited expression in sports and games. He extols cooperation and teamwork while harboring deeply antisocial impulses. He praises respect for rules and regulations in the secret belief that they do not apply to himself. Acquisitive in the sense that his cravings have no limits, he does not accumulate goods and provisions against the future, in the manner of the acquisitive individualist of nineteenth-century political economy, but demands immediate gratification and lives in a state of restless, perpetually unsatisfied desire.

The narcissist has no interest in the future because, in part, he has so little interest in the past. He finds it difficult to internalize happy associations or to create a store of loving memories with which to face the latter part of his life, which under the best of conditions always brings sadness and pain. In a narcissistic society—a society that gives increasing prominence and encouragement to narcissistic traits—the cultural devaluation of the past reflects not only the poverty of the prevailing ideologies, which have lost their grip on reality and abandoned the attempt to master it, but the poverty of the narcissist's inner life. A society that has made "nostalgia" a marketable commodity on the cultural exchange quickly repudiates the suggestion that life in the past was in any important way better than life today. Having trivialized the past by equating it with outmoded styles of consumption, discarded fashions and attitudes, people today resent anyone who draws on the past in serious discussions of contemporary conditions or attempts to use the past as a standard by which to judge the present. Current critical dogma equates every such reference to the past as itself an expression of nostalgia. As Albert Parr[3] has observed, this kind of reasoning "rules out entirely any insights gained, and any values arrived at by personal experience, since such experiences are always located in the past, and therefore in the precincts of nostalgia."

To discuss the complexities of our relation to the past under the heading of "nostalgia" substitutes sloganeering for the objective social criticism with which this attitude tries to associate itself. The fashionable sneer that now automatically greets every loving recollection of the past attempts to exploit the prejudices of a pseudoprogressive society on behalf of the status quo. But we now know—thanks to the work of Christopher Hill, E. P. Thompson,[4] and other historians—that many radical movements in the past have drawn strength and sustenance from the myth or memory of a golden age in the still more distant

---

[3]Lasch may have been referring to the author of *Art and Environment in an Age of Abundance* (1970).
[4]Prominent British historians.

past. This historical discovery reinforces the psychoanalytic insight that loving memories constitute an indispensable psychological resource in maturity, and that those who cannot fall back on the memory of loving relations in the past suffer terrible torments as a result. The belief that in some ways the past was a happier time by no means rests on a sentimental illusion; nor does it lead to a backward-looking, reactionary paralysis of the political will.

My own view of the past is just the opposite of David Donald's. Far from regarding it as a useless encumbrance, I see the past as a political and psychological treasury from which we draw the reserves (not necessarily in the form of "lessons") that we need to cope with the future. Our culture's indifference to the past—which easily shades over into active hostility and rejection—furnishes the most telling proof of that culture's bankruptcy. The prevailing attitude, so cheerful and forward-looking on the surface, derives from a narcissistic impoverishment of the psyche and also from an inability to ground our needs in the experience of satisfaction and contentment. Instead of drawing on our own experience, we allow experts to define our needs for us and then wonder why those needs never seem to be satisfied. "As people become apt pupils in learning how to need," Ivan Illich[5] writes, "the ability to shape wants from experienced satisfaction becomes a rare competence of the very rich or the seriously undersupplied."

For all these reasons, the devaluation of the past has become one of the most important symptoms of the cultural crisis to which this book addresses itself, often drawing on historical experience to explain what is wrong with our present arrangements. A denial of the past, superficially progressive and optimistic, proves on closer analysis to embody the despair of a society that cannot face the future.

[5]Cultural critic and author of *The Right to Useful Unemployment and Its Professional Enemies* (1978).

8

ROBERT BELLAH

Human Conditions for a Good Society

March 25, 1979

In this article, Bellah emphasized the deep roots of what he saw as problems afflicting contemporary America. What appealed to Carter was Bellah's contrast between an individualism based on market orientation and a commitment to a communal, public good grounded in historic and religious traditions.

... There were indeed [in America's formative period, from the 1630s to the 1850s] two partly incompatible models of the relation of individual and society that were deeply rooted in the American tradition. One model was the covenant, ... based on unlimited promise involving care and concern for others under divine law and judgment. In the covenant model people participate in each other's lives because they are mutually committed to values that transcend self-interest. The second model is the contract in which people join together to maximize self-interest and in which they stay together only as long as there is a fairly immediate "payoff." The covenant model was rooted in Biblical religion. The contract model was rooted in the market, in what came to be called capitalism, and in the ideology of individualistic liberalism that defended it.

... Even though nostalgia for Norman Rockwell's America runs deep, most Americans today sense that something has gone drastically wrong. Confidence in American institutions and in the American project, a confidence that could be taken for granted through most of our history, has become very problematic today. I think we can locate that break in the line of continuity that has led directly to our present perplexities in the decade of the 1960s.

The Vietnam War was not, I believe, the cause of that break but only its occasion, only the most vivid indication that we were not what

Robert Bellah, "Human Conditions for a Good Society," in "Ideas in Transition: Ideas in America," 100th anniv. ed., *St. Louis Post-Dispatch,* 25 Mar. 1979, 8–11.

we thought we were, that our ideas about ourselves no longer made sense of our reality, and that our future is uncertain indeed.

... In the past the covenant model had provided the context within which the contract model could operate. For without the presence of a general sense of basic trust in society even the market cannot exist. As Tocqueville, not to mention the founders of our republic, often pointed out, unrestrained self-interest will destroy the conditions of freedom in society and precipitate the coming of tyranny.

The classic theorists used the word "corruption" for that situation in which self-interest has become our sole concern and the major restraints on it, particularly religion and public participation, are no longer effective. . . . For the founders of our republic it [corruption] is the opposite of republican virtue; it is love of one's own good more than of the common good; it is the concern for oneself whatever happens to one's neighbor. Corruption is the thing that destroys republics.

Corruption, again using the eighteenth-century vocabulary, is to be found in luxury, dependence and ignorance. Luxury is that pursuit of material things that diverts us from concern for the public good, that leads us to exclusive concern for our own good, or what we would today call consumerism. Dependence naturally follows from luxury for it consists in accepting the dominance of whatever person or group, or, we might say today, governmental or private corporate structure, that promises us it will take care of our material desires. The welfare state—and here I refer to the welfare that goes to the great corporations, to most of us above the median income through special tax breaks, and the workers whose livelihood depends on an enormous military budget, as much as to the "welfare" that goes to the desperately poor to keep them from starving—the welfare state, then, in all of its prolixity, is the very type of what the eighteenth century meant by dependence. And finally ignorance, that is, political ignorance, is the result of luxury and dependence. It is a lack of interest in public things, a concern only for the private, a willingness to be governed by those who promise to take care of us even without our knowledgeable consent. . . .

Unfortunately the most prominent form of civil consciousness visible today is rather a form of corruption than an antidote to it. . . . A movement that claims to revive part of our heritage, though in peculiarly narrow and selfish form, has appeared. I refer to the middle-class tax revolt that would never have got as far as it has if the poor and the minorities had not so largely withdrawn from the electoral process in profound disillusion.[1] In the name of traditional American ideals of small government and self-help a significant sector of our middle class has decided that it does not choose to pay for the social costs of a reasonably decent society under the conditions of late industrial capitalism. The language of middle-class asceticism masks the rise of middle-class hedonism and what is really being said is that private consumerism is more important than the amenities of public life.

One can only say that the present narrow and mean-spirited mood of the middle class can but quickly be self-defeating. For with every kind of problem, ecological, economic, social and international, growing larger and threatening the very survival of the consumer economy and the privatism it fosters, major decisions in the public sphere and at the highest level will have to be taken. The world in which we live will simply not allow us the luxury of a purely negative demand for "small government." Now above all public confidence and commitment to the common good are necessary for our very survival. But the present mood betrays a desperation and even despair just below the surface that could result in the decisions that cannot forever be postponed being made in a mood of vindictiveness and repression rather than generosity of spirit, with the consequences that could lead to the end of free government in America.

. . . May we not yet ask whether there might not be some aspects of our present situation that could lead to a reinvigoration of our mores and a new sense of the importance of the covenant model to balance the present dominance of the contract model? I think the greatest opportunity exists in the growing realization that endless economic growth is not the answer to all our problems even if it were possible and now seems doubtful. If the rise of industrial capitalism, for all the benefits it has conferred, lies at the root of most of our problems then the faltering of the economy that has become evident since the early 1970s and that shows no early sign of change may prove an occasion for some profound reflections about the direction of America in the decades ahead. If alert Americans in large numbers begin to realize that "big government" is not the cause of our difficulties but only a symptom of a way of life that worships wealth and power, that makes economic profit the arbiter of all values and that delivers us into the tyranny of the bottom line, then it may be possible to re-examine our present institutions and the values they embody.

---

[1] In 1978, California voters had passed Proposition 13, which was the first in a series of efforts to limit taxes.

... A decentralization and democratization of our economic institutions, by whatever name it is called, is a key to the revitalization of our mores and our public life. Moving into a world of little or no economic growth without such decentralization and democratization would only precipitate a Hobbesian struggle between groups to see who can profit at the expense of whom, a struggle all too evident in our present politics.

But a major shift in the organization of our economic life, with all it would entail in our society, cannot be expected as a result of more technocratic or organizational manipulation. So great a change, overcoming not only entrenched ways of thinking, could only be brought about by some kind of change to cultural consciousness, one would almost have to say some kind of spiritual awakening. We are, whether we like it or not, going to have to face a world of increasing scarcity and simplicity, voluntary or involuntary. We can enter that world with bitterness and antagonism, with a concern to protect ourselves and our families whatever becomes of others. Or we can enter it with a renewed sense of what John Winthrop[2] meant when he said in 1630, "We must delight in each other, make others' conditions our own, rejoice together, mourn together, labor and suffer together, always having before our eyes ... our community as members of the same body."

To come to terms with what has happened to us in the last century in a way that allows us to regain in a new way the spiritual meaning and the public participation that characterized our formative period — that it seems to me is the only way to create a livable human environment in the decades ahead. ... Only the presence of a new sense of moral commitment can produce the time and space for such experimentation and such variety. Nor can America hope to solve the problems of the late twentieth century alone. Unless there is a decline in international tension and above all a decline in armaments no nation can expect to solve its problems, and the threat of nuclear catastrophe will grow to inescapable proportions.

Finally, we may ask whether there are in America the resources from which a moral renewal and a new birth of public courage and public happiness could come. Has what I have called the corruption of our society gone too far for any such renewal to occur? In my opinion there are such significant pockets of republican virtue and reservoirs of moral courage that there is at least a fighting chance that we might

---

[2]John Winthrop (1588–1649) was a founder and first governor of the Massachusetts Bay Colony.

rise to the coming challenges. The Watergate crisis gave evidence not only of startling moral corruption but also of significant displays of public virtue, from nightwatchmen to Supreme Court justices. I believe that in our churches, our voluntary associations, and our homes there is commitment to the good and not merely to one's own good. That commitment needs articulation and expression. The kind of leadership that Martin Luther King gave us in an earlier time of moral crisis is badly needed today. But it is by no means impossible that an alert and responsible citizenry will call forth such leadership again. Martin Luther King could only succeed because most Americans knew he was right. I believe most Americans today know that only sacrifice, love and concern for the common good will see us through the crises that lie ahead. It is up to us to make that moral knowledge effective in social consciousness and institutional transformation.

3

Debates within the Administration

In the spring and early summer of 1979, members of the Carter administration debated the choices the president faced. They did so against the background of explosive events across the nation and around the world. The discussions in the White House, fierce at times, were not merely academic. At stake was the fate of Carter's presidency and of the nation. The 1980 election was on the horizon, with Carter facing formidable challengers—Senator Ted Kennedy within the Democratic party and Ronald Reagan and John Connally (former governors of California and Texas, respectively) among the Republicans. The energy crisis—and the crisis in Carter's presidency—continued, but with renewed intensity. Rising inflation, interest rates, and gas prices were adversely affecting most American households. Sporadic violence had broken out at gas stations. People waited in long lines for gasoline that, if available, was costly. Long-haul truckers protested conditions that threatened to undermine their economic well-being. Carter's approval rating dipped to historic lows. On June 28, OPEC raised prices once again. On July 1, the president returned from a long trip to Europe and Asia, physically exhausted but aware that he had to respond to the energy crisis gripping the nation. Three days later, on Independence Day, Carter took the advice of his wife and pollster Patrick Caddell and canceled the speech he was scheduled to deliver on July 5. In seclusion at Camp David, he held a national domestic summit that lasted for ten days.

In this period stretching from late June to mid-July, an intense, momentous, and often acrimonious debate occurred among the president's advisers. On one side stood Caddell, who shared with Carter a sense that profound moral and spiritual issues lay at the heart of the crisis the president and the nation faced. Much of the discussion swirled around Caddell's advice—both to cancel the July 5 speech and how to craft the one scheduled for July 15.

Within the administration, the primary opposition to Caddell came from Vice President Walter Mondale, domestic policy adviser Stuart Eizenstat, and media adviser Gerald Rafshoon. Their advice had its own intellectual antecedents, in the writings of political scientists Theodore Lowi, James MacGregor Burns, and Robert Dahl. Mondale and Eizenstat believed that the liberalism based on interest groups that had sustained the Democratic party since the mid-1930s now paralyzed American democracy. To some extent agreeing with Daniel Bell, Caddell, and Carter, they concluded that the way groups pursued self-interest undermined the quest for the public good. For example, environmentalists opposed nuclear energy, while labor unions supported it; those who spoke for the poor preferred price controls, while most in the business community wanted free markets. Such tensions, they believed, ensured that Carter would face fundamental structural impediments in any effort to restore a sense of national community and confidence in the presidency.

As Mondale, Eizenstat, and others offered advice to Carter, they urged him not to accuse the American people of moral weakness and instead to emphasize the difficult, practical situations Americans faced as they tried to balance their household budgets and purchase energy at reasonable prices. Whereas Caddell's view was pessimistic, even apocalyptic, Mondale and his allies preferred that the president strike an optimistic note. Reducing inflation was essential if Carter was to regain the voters' confidence. They kept their eyes on what Kennedy and Reagan might say on the campaign trail, rather than focusing their minds on what Tocqueville and Lasch had written. To Mondale and others, compassion for less fortunate members of society and a pragmatic approach were essential. They wanted a president who offered leadership, not sermons.

Born in 1928, Walter Mondale had grown up in an atmosphere of New Deal liberalism and midwestern progressivism. He earned his undergraduate and law degrees from the University of Minnesota, then cut his political teeth on the special brand of politics shaped by the influence of the Farmer-Labor party on the state's Democratic party. This tradition was best represented by Hubert Humphrey, Lyndon Johnson's vice president and the Democrats' presidential nominee in 1968. Throughout his adult life, Mondale took a liberal position on issues that mattered most to him—civil rights, unemployment, poverty, and education. He served as Minnesota attorney general from 1960 to 1964, when he was appointed to fill Humphrey's U.S. Senate seat when Humphrey became vice president. Mondale was elected to the Senate in 1966 and 1972, leaving to become vice president in 1976. Though not fully apparent at the time, Carter and Mondale represented two diverging trends in the Democratic party, with the president pointing forward to his fellow southerner Bill Clinton's embrace of a centrist politics and the vice president standing in the storied liberal tradition that went back to Franklin Roosevelt and forward to Ted Kennedy. Carter, who placed efficiency ahead of equity, was willing to cut social programs such as aid to public schools and Social Security to balance the federal budget. Mondale, with struggling workers and farmers in the Midwest and African Americans in cities on his mind, wanted a government that used social programs to improve the lives of people most adversely affected by rampant inflation, high fuel costs, and threatened social programs.

In the spring and summer of 1979, Mondale was despondent. Like vice presidents before him, he had to defend his president's policies, even though he neither shaped nor believed in them. Personally loyal to the president yet concerned over what he saw as Carter's political ineptitude and departure from liberal positions, Mondale seriously considered resigning from the vice presidency in late May 1979. At the Camp David meetings in early July, Mondale fought vigorously as he tried to convince the president to reject Caddell's approach.

In these battles, one of Mondale's most important allies was Stuart Eizenstat. Born in 1943, he had earned his B.A. at the University of North Carolina and his law degree at Harvard. He had served on the White House staff in the last years of the Johnson administration and on Hubert Humphrey's campaign staff in 1968. He came to know Carter when he practiced law in Atlanta. Throughout Carter's presidency, he was the president's senior domestic policy adviser. In the debates over energy policy, Eizenstat opposed Caddell's advice that the president tell the American people that they were suffering from a spiritual malaise that was sapping their moral fiber.

9

STUART EIZENSTAT

Memo to the President

June 28, 1979

Carter's senior domestic policy adviser wrote to the president as Carter was heading to the Tokyo summit, a meeting of leading industrial nations in late June. Eizenstat apprised the president of the dire situation he would face when he returned to the United States several days later: truckers on strike to pressure the government to let them fill their gas tanks; citizens frustrated by long lines at gas stations and by inflation that eroded their finances; and members of Congress anxious about having to face their constituents.

MEMORANDUM FOR: THE PRESIDENT

FROM: STU EIZENSTAT

SUBJECT: Energy

Since you left for Japan, the domestic energy problem has continued to worsen:

— The actions taken to help the truckers have not yet broken the back of the strike. Jack[1] and I are continuing to review the problem. As you know, the Vice President will today announce a series of actions to help improve the situation.
— Gas lines are growing throughout the Northeast and are spreading to the Midwest.
— Sporadic violence over gasoline continues to occur. A recent incident in Pennsylvania injured 40.

---

[1]Jack Watson was on the White House staff as assistant to the president for intergovernment affairs.

Stuart Eizenstat to Jimmy Carter, Memorandum, 28 June 1979, Office of Staff Secretary: Presidential Handwriting File, box 137, folder "Trip to Japan and Korea, 6/22/79–7/1/79 [1]," JCPL.

— Gasoline station operators are threatening a nationwide strike unless DOE[2] grants an emergency profit margin increase.

— The latest CPI[3] figures have demonstrated how substantially energy is affecting inflation—gasoline prices have risen 55% since January.

— Congress is growing more nervous by the day over the energy problem. The Moorhead bill[4] was pushed through the House yesterday, so Members could go home for the recess claiming to have done something about the problem. It is fair to say that in normal times, a bill as significant as Moorhead's would have been considered much more carefully. Despite that vote, and the forthcoming vote on Thursday on the windfall tax, Members are literally afraid to go home over the recess, for fear of having to deal with very angry constituents. That fear was expressed to the Vice President and me yesterday when we briefed Members on the Tokyo Summit. They were almost completely uninterested in the Summit, and spent all of two hours talking about gasoline and related problems.

— Press accounts are starting to appear about the Administration's inability to deliver on the commitment to have 240 million barrels of distillate[5] in stock by October. The Northeast will soon be pressuring us to clarify whether we still believe 240 is possible.

— The continuing problem of conflicting signals and numbers from DOE persists. The DOE gasoline allocation formulas are now coming under particularly heavy attack. Yesterday, the State of Maryland sued DOE for misallocating gasoline. Other States can be expected to shortly follow that politically popular route.

In sum, we have a worsening short-term domestic energy crisis, and I do not expect to see (with the possible exception of a break in the truckers' strike) any improvement by the time you return.

I do not need to detail for you the political damage we are suffering from all of this. It is perhaps sufficient to say that nothing which has occurred in the Administration to date—not the Soviet agreement

[2]Department of Energy.
[3]Consumer price index, the government's standard measurement of prices.
[4]William S. Moorhead (D-Pa.) sponsored a House bill to develop synthetic fuels.
[5]Oil distillates are a by-product of the refining process.

on the Middle East, not the Lance[6] matter, not the Panama Canal Treaties, not the defeat of several major domestic legislative proposals, not the sparring with Kennedy, and not even double-digit inflation—have added so much water to our ship. Nothing else has so frustrated, confused, angered the American people—or so targeted their distress at you personally, as opposed to your advisors, or Congress, or outside interests. Mayor Koch[7] indicated to me (during a meeting the Vice President and I had with the New York Congressional delegation on their gas problems) he had not witnessed anything comparable to the current emotion in American political life since Vietnam.

While the Vietnam analogy is a strained one in many ways, it is one which this week press accounts are beginning to make. The similarities between problems of credibility and political opposition from the left are real, though clearly undeserved. We can expect to see repetition in coming weeks of the analogy, which was relevant at the ADA[8] convention I addressed over the weekend.

All of this is occurring at a particularly inopportune time. Inflation is higher than ever. A recession is clearly facing us. (Indeed, when our July budget forecast comes out with a zero GNP[9] estimate we should not attempt to avoid the obvious, as Ford tried to do, but we should be honest and admit a recession is likely.) OPEC is raising prices once again. The polls are lower than they have ever been. (The latest Harris poll shows something never before seen—a Republican opponent, Reagan, leading you by several points.) Kennedy's popularity appears at a peak. And the Congress seems completely beyond anyone's control.

In many respects, this would appear to be the worst of times. But I honestly believe we can change this to a time of opportunity. We have a better opportunity than ever before to assert leadership over an apparently insolvable problem, to shift the cause for inflation and energy problems to OPEC, to gain credibility with the American people, to offer hope of an eventual solution, to regain our political losses. We

---

[6]Bert Lance, a close associate of Carter's from Georgia and director of the Office of Management and Budget, was embroiled in a scandal over his personal and business affairs.

[7]Ed Koch, mayor of New York City.

[8]Americans for Democratic Action was an organization of liberals who constituted an important part of the Democratic coalition.

[9]An estimate that the economy would not grow.

should seize this opportunity now and with all our skill. If we fail to do so, the late hour may foreclose a similar opportunity again coming our way.

My recommendations for how to do this, many of which I have discussed previously with you and separately with Ham and Jody,[10] are as follows:

1. Use the OPEC price increase as the occasion to mark the beginning of our new approach to energy. It must be said by you—and by us—time and again publicly to be a watershed event. We must turn the increase to our advantage by clearly pointing out its devastating economic impact and as the justification for our efforts against the OPEC cartel and for increased domestic production of all types. We have provided you with a tough statement that will accomplish those ends, and buy us a week or so before the public will expect more specifics. I urge you to use that statement and to keep it as strong as possible. A statement which goes light on OPEC or a commitment to synthetics and other domestic initiatives will not convince the public that anything is different, that we are embarking on a new effort, or that there is hope that the energy problem will be solved, or that we will ever stand up to OPEC (which Americans want even more than cheap gasoline).

2. Your decision to eliminate or cut short your Hawaii stop vividly demonstrates your commitment to dig into this problem without delay.

3. When you return, and before you go to Camp David, you should at least hold one full day of meetings at the White House to consult with your advisors about the various energy problems, to assess the Summit, to report to those Congressional leaders in town, and to determine how and when you should report to the public. A full day's work on energy with your advisors would be helpful to us to get our signals and orders straight, but also to demonstrate your continuing commitment to solving this problem.

4. That one day or so of energy events cannot be allowed to pass without repeated follow-on events when you return from Camp David. Every day you need to be dealing with—and publicly be seen as dealing with—the major energy problems now facing us. Unless the attention to energy is almost total during the two [to] three weeks after

[10]Hamilton Jordan and Jody Powell.

your return, we will *not* turn the course of events around, and certainly we will not convince the American people that we have a firmer grasp on the problem than they now perceive.

Your enormous success in the Middle East peace process was due, to a very large degree, to your personal, constant involvement over a sustained period of time. The energy situation is different in many ways than the Middle East, but the need for you to stay the course, to demand answers, to convince others of the need to act and to compromise, and to control the competing forces within the government is very similar. With that type of involvement, we can regain the initiative and rise above much of the confusion and bureaucratic tangling now occurring.

We can arrange a schedule of events that are meaningful and worthwhile during this period.

5. You must address the enormous credibility and management problems of DOE which equal in public perception those which State or Defense had during Vietnam (whether fairly or not). We can discuss this in detail upon your return.

6. Shortly after you return, we will have a memorandum for you to decide how to propose spending the funds raised by the windfall tax. That memorandum will include the results of a comprehensive interagency review now underway to examine the synfuels[11] issue and develop a significant proposal for you to announce. Once you decide the direction you want these new production initiatives to take, you might consider a major address to the nation. That address could review the energy situation, explain the causes of current problems, and announce our new initiatives. The address would be around the third week of July.

7. In addition to the synfuels and energy production announcement, I believe we should announce separately the creation of a National Energy Mobilization Board. Such a Board would be designated to select energy projects—like pipelines, port facilities or research and development facilities—which are to be built in the national interest, eliminating all of the normal regulatory tangle that slows such projects down. During World War II, we had such a Board to get warrelated projects expedited. This Board would be modeled after the

[11] Synthetic fuels.

World War II example. I have asked DOE to staff this out and have explored the idea quietly within the Administration and on the Hill and have found an enormous receptivity. Your announcing the creation of this Board would confirm your intention to treat this matter as one of highest national security.

8. You have a variety of speeches scheduled after your return—the Governors, NACO, Operation PUSH, CWA.[12] Each of those occasions should be used to talk about energy. That is the only subject the public wants to hear about and we should use those opportunities to get our message across repeatedly. The windfall tax campaign was successful because of your repeated discussion of it during a short period of time. That success can be repeated through these speech opportunities.

With strong steps we can mobilize the nation around a real crisis and with a clear enemy—OPEC.

[12]NACO = National Association of Counties; Operation PUSH was the civil rights and antipoverty organization led by Jesse Jackson; CWA = Communications Workers of America, a labor union.

10

ESTHER PETERSON

Energy Conservation Program:
Memo to the President
June 28, 1979

Esther Peterson, the president's special assistant for consumer affairs, had a long and distinguished career as an activist on labor, women's, and consumer issues. Here, as the federal government's chief representative of consumers, she advocated the politically charged policy of rationing gasoline.

Esther Peterson to Jimmy Carter, Memorandum, "Energy Conservation Program," 28 June 1979, Office of Staff Secretary: Presidential Handwriting File, box 137, folder "7/3/79," JCPL.

MEMORANDUM FOR: THE PRESIDENT

FROM: ESTHER PETERSON

SUBJECT: Energy Conservation Program

We need an energy conservation program which consumers will support, and one potential answer is to resubmit our gas rationing plan to Congress.

When Congress rejected the original rationing plan, it did so at a time when no one had tangible evidence that the gas shortage is real. While Americans are still skeptical about the shortage, the simple truth is that gasoline and home heating oil will be in short supply for years to come. With the prospect of long gas lines and cold winters staring consumers in the face, an equitable rationing may now be a more attractive alternative.

Reintroduction of the rationing plan has several positive consequences:

1. It conveys to the public a sense that you are taking decisive action to assure order and an equitable distribution of the petroleum supplies that we have. In so doing, it also puts the onus on Congress' back.
2. Rationing would immediately reduce gas consumption and perhaps diminish the threat of a recession in the U.S.
3. It would demonstrate to the world, on the heels of the Tokyo Summit, that you are taking decisive action to assure that the United States is fulfilling its international responsibilities.
4. It would lessen the inevitable adverse impact on our balance of payments that will result from the OPEC price increases.

Given the public's skepticism about the origin of the shortages, other voluntary conservation measures are not likely to result in significant fuel savings. Rapidly escalating fuel prices have not diminished consumers' thirst for gasoline and a "me first" attitude for the supplies that are available is prevalent within each sector of the economy. While it may not be popular, the general equity inherent in rationing may be more preferable than the general disorder that now prevails. I urge you to resubmit the rationing proposal to Congress.

11

ACHSAH NESMITH, WALTER SHAPIRO, AND GORDON STEWART

Energy Speech: Memo to Gerald Rafshoon and Hendrik Hertzberg

June 29, 1979

Three speechwriters for the president—Achsah Nesmith, Walter Shapiro, and Gordon Stewart—sent this memo to Gerald Rafshoon, an Atlanta advertising executive who coordinated Carter's media efforts, and Hendrik Hertzberg, a presidential speechwriter who was later an editor at the New Yorker. *They were all concerned that the president, still involved in international diplomacy, might not realize the seriousness of the domestic situation he would find on his return home a few days later.*

The mood in the country is grim. People are mad—fighting mad. The situation has deteriorated alarmingly since the President left for Japan. We are writing this memo to express our collective concern that unless the President adopts a firm, consistent and believable tone on energy, beginning the moment he gets off the plane, the political damage may be irreparable.

Gas lines promote anger, not conservation. Hatred for the oil companies is only matched by lack of confidence in the Administration. People will accept rationing because it implies fairness; "allocations" is a word that suggests special privileges for those who scream the loudest. The OPEC price rise and Administration predictions of 800,000 people losing their jobs all inspire fears of a deep recession as bad as 1974–75 or even worse. The independent truckers strike is just further evidence that the social fabric is crumbling. It is futile to guarantee farmers fuel to plant and harvest if they can't get crops to market. It's absurd to talk about increasing exports if factories are closing down because of the truckers strike.

Rationally, the country is not in dire straits, but what has fed the

Achsah Nesmith, Walter Shapiro, and Gordon Stewart to Gerald Rafshoon and Hendrik Hertzberg, Memorandum, "Energy Speech," 29 June 1979, Speechwriters: Chronological File, box 50, folder "7/15/79, Proposed Remarks on Energy [2]," JCPL.

current mood is the fear things will grow much worse *soon* and that if we are incapable of mastering our current problems we will be overwhelmed by the problems to come.

No one understands why all these things are happening *now.* People sitting in gas lines think their inconvenience is pointless. No one understands what the Administration's energy policy is, and how it will help, all they know is that the President has made an awful lot of television speeches on energy—*and things have gotten worse.*

We strongly advise against another televised energy speech—unless the President has a bold, new, and ambitious policy to announce. People want action on energy. They do not want Presidential preaching or the Administration piously saying, "We told you so, but you didn't listen to us."

The first priority is to convince people that something is being done. We must end the image of drift, confusion and vacillation. From the moment he gets off the plane, the President, in every public appearance, should convey an image of somber concern. There should be no jokes, no overtly political moves, no sense that this is business as usual. It may be advisable for the President to halt all public political activity until the crisis is under control. The American people want firmness and leadership, they are worrying about gas lines and the disruption of our economy—*not the 1980 election.* Anything we do about energy must have bipartisan and Congressional support.

Another energy speech is *not* the way to convince people something is being done. We have just had two foreign summits that too few people care about. We need a domestic summit on energy that everybody cares about, and one where every participant is under pressure to accept common programs. *Then, and only then, should there be an energy speech.*

This summit should be announced on arrival in Washington without a long speech. The President should immediately project a grim determination to turn this situation around. Any further delay, any more contradictory signals on energy, will be fatal.

If, however, an energy speech is to be made next week, we have the following cautions on what must be avoided:

— There should not be a defensive or preachy tone. Defending the Administration's record will only make people madder; what is needed is a new tone that implies a break with the past.

— Under no circumstances should there be any hint that gasoline lines should be accepted or justified as a way of encouraging conservation. The inconvenience of gasoline lines is pointless and infuriating. What further defeats conservation is that in many parts of the country, gas-guzzlers can still get all the fuel they need. Rationing is better than gas lines. If not rationing, some national program to distribute gasoline supplies fairly.

—There should not be any overdrawn appeals for individual conservation efforts. Fewer lectures, less father-to-child stuff, and more positive motivation. People will conserve if their efforts are perceived as fitting into a coherent national policy. Without a coherent policy, appeals for conservation have all the emotional force of "only *you* can prevent forest fires."

—All discussions of alternative energy should be made as tangible as possible. Code words like "synthetic fuels" sound vague and visionary. If war is the analogy for energy, let's fight it with clear targets and victories. Let's not make alternative energy sound as dull as a protracted antitrust suit.

—No more berating the American people for waste and selfishness. What can be more wasteful than sitting in a two-hour gas line in a country with lagging productivity or driving around looking for an open gas station, burning fuel.

—The next energy speech—no matter when it is given—may be our last chance to reach the American people. *It is hard to get the American people to listen now; it will be impossible if the situation deteriorates further.*

Any energy speech must be absolutely honest. If the supply problem is Iran, we must say so. If the supply problem is the result of the oil companies deliberately withholding supplies, we must say so. If the government doesn't have the answers now, we must immediately take steps to get them. People are still willing to make sacrifices *if* they believe they have been told the whole truth and those sacrifices are rational and shared equally and fairly.

We cannot stick to the same themes we have used for the last two years. *The situation has changed.* An energy speech must be different in tone, emphasis and content from any we have given before. More of the same is a formula for political disaster.

We need the broadest-based broadest-minded course of action that is both specific and visionary. We can announce it anytime, anyplace. *After we have decided to act.*

12

HAMILTON JORDAN

Memo to the President

July 3, 1979

Hamilton Jordan was part of Carter's inner circle and one of his most trusted advisers. Soon after the speech of July 15, 1979, Jordan became Carter's chief of staff. Though in some ways siding with Caddell, he also offered his own analysis, which had resonance among contemporary policy analysts: Can a democracy function in a crisis if it is "increasingly pluralistic" and "politically fragmented," with competing interest groups undermining the public good?

TO: PRESIDENT CARTER

FROM: HAMILTON JORDAN

RE: Thursday Night Speech

I thought that I would be doing you a disservice if I did not alert you to the fact that there is some soul-searching and second-guessing about the wisdom of your Thursday night speech. Pat Caddell is the "ringleader" of those who think that it might be a mistake.

After hearing the subsequent discussions and talking to various persons, I am thoroughly convinced that the Thursday night speech of the type we discussed is highly desirable and very necessary.

Let me make several points:

1. You are *perceived* by the American people as having been out of the country for most of the past month working on issues and problems that are not "their" priorities right now.
2. Unfair as it may seem, the Tokyo Summit which was a significant energy victory for our country and the Western democracies was viewed by people here at home as being

---

Hamilton Jordan to Jimmy Carter, Memorandum, "Thursday Night Speech," 3 July 1979, Chief of Staff: Jordan, box 37, folder "Speech, President's, 7/15/79," JCPL.

91

irrelevant to the problems faced by the people here at home. One network had interviews with people in gas lines asking about your trip to Tokyo. The typical response was, "what in the hell is Carter doing in Japan and Korea when all the problems are here at home?" Another person said that it didn't make any difference where their President was as he was helpless to deal with the problem anyway.

3. I believe that it would have been a considerable mistake for you to have waited too long before saying something to the American people about energy after having been out of the country for most of the month when the problem finally seemed to penetrate the consciousness of the American people. Certainly we will be saying once again some of the same things that you have said many times before to the American people. The difference will be that in the past your warnings of dire consequences were made in an irrelevant atmosphere when people were not concerned about energy. When you say them today, they will be said in a relevant atmosphere when people are finally focused on the problem.

4. Phil Wise[1] called me yesterday from Florida. He has taken a week's vacation and has been traveling around the state seeing our friends. Phil said some very pertinent things. Phil said that the gravity of the problem had begun to sink in, that people were beginning to realize that the problem might be both serious and permanent, and that they were mostly confused by conflicting forecasts about the future. But most of all, Phil reports, the people that he has been meeting with (even those that are mad at us) *want to hear from their President.* They want the facts and even though they are cynical and mad, there is still the feeling in the country that you will tell them the truth.

5. I believe that the American people would like to feel that you understand and can identify with their own frustrations and fears. That is the reason that I feel strongly that a long delay in addressing the American people will only contribute to the psychological panic in the country and further damage us politically.

Without presuming to speak for Pat Caddell, let me attempt to state his concerns. Pat continues to argue that we need first to make our

---

[1]The coordinator of Carter's 1976 presidential campaign in Florida.

"America is going to hell speech" to grab the attention of the American people and then to focus their attention on the energy problems. Pat argues that in the present atmosphere people are so alienated from you and turned off that we will have great difficulty getting their attention. He thinks that your attacking the larger and more abstract problem should come before you address the country on energy.

Pat is right that we are not in an ideal posture at the present time to rally the American people. We are low in the polls and a lot of people have turned us off and given up on us. *But we cannot not speak out and not attempt to lead just because people may not listen to us and may not follow.* We have no choice but to try. The energy problem symbolizes all of the problems that face our society: During a time of crisis can a democracy that is increasingly pluralistic, politically fragmented and dispirited about its future be united to face a problem that is a challenge to its economic and political greatness? I would argue that the energy problem is the perfect "hook" on which to make the other points about the crisis of spirit which faces our people. I think we were all nervous and searching for a way previously for you to make a speech such as Pat suggested and make it relevant and have it taken seriously by the American people. The energy crisis makes it relevant.

I never get involved in speechwriting, but I would like to make several points about the tone of your speech Thursday:

1. "I wish that I could stand before you tonight and assure you that everything is going to be a lot better, but I can't. The energy crisis that I have talked with you about on ____ occasions is now with us and will not just go away."

2. "We have a long-term problem which we must all work now to solve for the sake of our children and future generations. In the short term, we have a real and genuine shortage which you and I working together must manage without disrupting the economic and social fabric of our country."

3. Some reference should be made to July the 4th and our country's independence which has been fought for and reaffirmed on battlefields all over the world. That we are fighting now for our economic independence and until we win it back, our lives and future will be shaped and controlled by people and circumstances that we cannot control or even influence.

4. While holding out hope for the future and pointing to the light at the end of the tunnel, you should avoid statements that sound too optimistic. In fact, in all future statements, we

should err on the side of caution, pessimism or "we are not
sure—there are too many variables."

Finally, I have no illusions that this speech will solve all of our problems. It will probably be panned by the media for lacking enough substance. *But, if in the present atmosphere, you can finally focus the
attention of the American people on the root causes for the problem and
point to the way out, you will have established a foundation on which we
can build in the weeks and months ahead. The speech is badly needed.*

13

WALTER MONDALE

Energy Speech: Memo to the President

July 4, 1979

*In this memo, Vice President Mondale was responding to several drafts
of the speech scheduled for July 5 that Carter canceled. Mondale provided
the most articulate opposition to the approach Caddell and others urged
the president to follow, here warning Carter to praise rather than blame
the American people and to remember that Americans faced tangible
problems that politicians could address rather than vague and spiritual
ones that were beyond remedy by the political process.*

MEMORANDUM FOR: THE PRESIDENT

FROM: THE VICE PRESIDENT

SUBJECT: Energy Speech

I have just seen draft two of the energy speech. I have recently tried
several energy themes in various parts of the country, and I believe I
know which approaches are getting the best response.

Walter Mondale to Jimmy Carter, Memorandum, "Energy Speech," 4 July 1979, Walter
F. Mondale Papers, 149.5.15.6 (F), Manuscript Collection, Minnesota Historical Society,
St. Paul, Minn.

The draft speech in its present form sounds too much like an old scold and a grouch. Instead of scolding the public we should play to their better instincts, and I think that will bring forth the best response.

We should say: Americans know well how to deal with a crisis in a mature and responsible way. After the shock has passed, where staggered hours, minimum purchase rules and odd-even systems have been used to break gasoline lines, people are conserving and increasingly using mass transportation, carpooling and other methods of cutting energy waste.

We can make clear that for some time these problems will continue to flare up but we are doing several things that will help to ease the crisis:

— switching to natural gas
— pressing for maximum refinery production
— improving the allocations system
— and giving the Governors the power to see that service stations follow staggered hours and that systems are adopted to discourage panic buying.

We should say that one of the reasons we have a problem is the need to rebuild home heating oil because we cannot ask poor people or old people to freeze this winter for lack of home heating oil.

Then I would go after OPEC, hitting them on the latest price increase and saying that this is the final straw. It shows the cost of being overly dependent on foreign sources of oil. It aggravates inflation, it increases unemployment, it slows economic growth and it threatens our security and independence.

One of the strongest things you can do is to praise American natural and human resources.

We are incredibly blessed with natural resources: in our vast reserves of coal, oil shale, unconventional gas and in our potential to harness solar energy and bio-mass, including gasahol. We have several Saudi Arabias in oil shale alone.

We are even more blessed with human resources: the highly skilled men and women in our workforce, the best scientists and engineers, trained and experienced business leadership, and above all in our national will to overcome the energy crisis.

There is a way to match our natural and human resources, and to mobilize them to secure our country's energy future. We can do it. We did it with the Manhattan project. We did it with synthetic rubber during World War II. We did it with the Apollo project. And once again we will do it with energy and America will show the world that there is a way out of this crisis.

We will establish a new and independent corporation to produce synthetic fuels. We will create an Energy Mobilization Board.

We will pursue every approach that makes sense:

— stepping up use of coal
— producing synthetic fuels
— carrying out the most aggressive solar program in the industrialized world.

We will produce natural gas as well as oil from Alaska and build the pipelines and the refineries needed to produce and deliver supplies to consuming markets.

We are engaged in negotiations with Mexico on natural gas and other energy matters, and we will prepare an agreement that benefits our two countries.

But the American people should not be taxed twice: first through runaway OPEC imposed prices, and second to pay for the public investment needed to develop new energy supplies. The windfall tax will do two things: it would take unearned profits that otherwise would be spent elsewhere and use them to massively increase our ability to produce American energy supplies.

I would then close with a strong Fourth of July independence passage making clear that this generation of Americans will stand up to and overcome the energy crisis.

In my judgment Americans will respond well over the short term if we give them a reason for hope over the long term. We can be candid and honest but we should be affirmative.

Finally, I would recommend that we condense the discussion of the problem, the causes and the facts about the situation we face today, and use numbers that explain the problem clearly, in terms people can understand. I would use gallons of gasoline per driver rather than hundreds of thousands of barrels of oil and try to keep this section crisp.

14

MARSHALL LOEB

How to Counter OPEC

July 9, 1979

Marshall Loeb's advice to Carter, offered as a senior editor of Time *rather than as a member of the administration, captured some of the choices the president faced. At the same time, it reflected indecisiveness about how to decide what path to pursue.*

Can anything be done to break the tyranny of the toughest cartel in history, to prevent oil shortages and price gouging? The answer is yes—*if.* If the U.S. is ready. At last, the jarring events of the past few weeks have probably persuaded Americans that the crisis is real, and that the nation can meet it by making some sacrifices and changes in its life-style, by taking some chances and paying some costs. What is needed, of course, is to lessen immediately the country's umbilical dependence on crude oil from the cartel. Slackened demand could loosen the market, make OPEC nervous and start a rush by its members to sell. The ways to accomplish that are well known and many, for there is no single miracle stroke against OPEC.

Because nearly 40% of all oil used in the nation goes for gasoline, the first and most important step is to brake gasoline demand. Rationing would seem to be the politically expedient method. A *New York Times–CBS News* poll in early June found that three out of five Americans would prefer rationing to shortages and skyrocketing prices. Yet any form of rationing would tend to be inequitable and a bureaucratic nightmare. Even during World War II, when the U.S. was united as never before or since, gasoline rationing was marked by corruption, favoritism and loopholes. Today, rationing would be enforced by the same Department of Energy folks who have done so much to confuse and compound the gasoline mess. Says Treasury Secretary Michael Blumenthal: "The more I'm in the Government, the more market-oriented I become. No bureaucrats with pins at the Department of

Marshall Loeb, "How to Counter OPEC," *Time,* 9 July 1979, 23.

Energy, trying to figure out how much gasoline each gas station in the country should get, can set out a way to distribute gas in this country." Nor can they fairly and soundly figure out how much gas each driver needs and should get.

The House in May rejected the President's stand-by rationing plan, but it offers some clues to any future program. Car owners would get ration coupons and could sell unused coupons on a "white market" at any price; each car would be allotted about 50 gal. a month, though the totals would vary by state; no more than three cars in each household could receive coupons; extra rations would be given to police cars, ambulances, taxis, farm tractors; heavy recreational vehicles would get nothing.

Probably a more efficient measure would be to "ration by price," that is, to free the market and remove gasoline price controls. President Carter has the authority to do that, subject to congressional veto. Decontrol would cause a political storm because prices would immediately rise. Some experts warn that gasoline would soar to $2 a gal., but free market advocates argue that long-term prices would go up much less, by perhaps a few cents or a dime a gal. In any case, three facts are most significant. First, a free market unquestionably would reduce demand by raising the cost. Second, the price would still be lower in the U.S. than in any other industrial nation except Canada. Third, the Government could use taxes both to skim off any "windfall" profits and to compensate lower-income people, who must otherwise be hurt by higher gasoline costs.

It has become a commonplace that America has scarcely begun to conserve. Small, voluntary steps can add up to major savings. A driver can save about 5% of the gas he normally uses by keeping his tires properly inflated and another 10% by keeping his engine in tune. A householder can save 15% on his heating bill, and 7.5% on his air-conditioning bill, simply by keeping his storm windows on all year.

But the largest savings will have to come from a combination of more tax incentives for buying home insulation, wood-burning furnaces and other oil-conserving devices, and much stiffer mandatory conservation rules. A number of innovative companies, including DuPont, AT&T and General Motors, have reduced their energy use relative to their output by 17% to 30% since the Arab oil embargo of 1973; yet many more firms have gone on giddily wasting energy. Consider the beneficial effects of a 20% surtax on the commercial use of electricity: skyscrapers that are lit up all night long and advertising signs that glisten at 4 A.M. would be turned off.

The nation will have to make the most of its available alternatives to oil, and to do that it will have to moderate some of its stringent environmental protection laws. The U.S. is the Saudi Arabia of coal, but a maze of regulations retard the mining, transportation and burning of coal, greatly inflating its price.

Many power-generating companies would switch from oil to coal if the U.S. removed the need for expensive scrubbers on plants that use low-sulfur Western coal. The U.S. also has to dig more coal mines (including strip mines), build more and safer nuclear plants, construct more oil refineries, drill more offshore wells, develop more oil shale projects. All of these will require some trade-offs with antipollution laws, and none of the projects can be accomplished if small groups of zealots set out to block them while OPEC's new Midases sit back and applaud.

The U.S. could also reduce OPEC's power by buying more oil and gas from nations outside the cartel, especially those in the Americas. The need is urgent to create a North American Common Market. Canada has vast supplies of natural gas; the U.S. could negotiate to provide guaranteed markets and much needed capital in return for a steady supply of gas. Mexico is proud and sensitive about its patrimony of oil and gas, but the U.S. could acquire more of it by admitting more Mexican immigrants, giving trade preferences to Mexican exports, exchanging American agricultural technology to help feed one of the world's fastest growing populations and generally treating its neighbor as an equal partner.

Salvation ultimately lies in developing alternative energies, but that will take many years. At OPEC's new prices, oil from the almost limitless supplies of U.S. shale now becomes competitive, but shale oil probably will not be available in quantity until 1990. Solar technology also has large promise but is still in its swaddling clothes. Two of the most promising alternatives for quick use are methane, which can be produced from garbage or manure, and alcohol, which can be made from grain and almost any other organic matter. The manufacture of both should be encouraged through tax incentives. Connecticut Senator Abraham Ribicoff has introduced a sensible bill that would require that 20% of all gasoline sold in the U.S. must come from oil alternatives.

Having done almost nothing in the six years since the Arab oil embargo, the Congress, roused at last, is considering no fewer than five major bills to subsidize the multibillion-dollar development of alternative energies. In the process of hurry-up and waste, much of the money will go down ratholes. But some of the subsidies will produce breakthroughs, just as urgent drives put men on the moon exactly ten years ago. Like it or not, the U.S. is now involved in a new war for independence. The only way it can win is to be prepared to conserve, convert, compromise and develop.

15

GERALD RAFSHOON

Memo to the President

July 10, 1979

Gerald Rafshoon, an Atlanta advertising executive who coordinated the media efforts for the president, prompted reporters to coin the term "rafshoonery" to refer to his efforts to spin the president's image. Here he weighed in against Caddell's approach even as he made clear how attuned he was to the imperatives of a media-saturated society.

MEMORANDUM TO: THE PRESIDENT

FROM: JERRY RAFSHOON

For the last few days, I have been compiling speech suggestions from everyone connected with this problem—from the extreme optimism of the Vice-President to Stu's desire to have a very substantive speech to Pat's apocalyptic first draft. I know that you are getting mixed signals from everyone and since I am supposed to coordinate this exercise, I will give you my final thoughts on the forthcoming address to the nation.

I also enclose a copy of Kirbo's[1] suggestions. They are good. I

[1] Charles Kirbo was an Atlanta lawyer who served, informally, as a presidential adviser.

Gerald Rafshoon to Jimmy Carter, Memorandum, 10 July 1979, Speechwriters: Chronological File, box 50, folder "7/15/79 Address to the Nation—Energy/Crisis of Confidence [1]," JCPL.

frankly think that if we give the speech that Caddell has proposed, it will be counterproductive to what we are trying to do. It could even be a disaster. When we sat up here last Thursday, after the initial shock of cancelling the July 5th speech, we were all grasping for straws and Pat's idea certainly was the foremost offered. Since that time, with the promise of a new beginning coming down daily from the mountain top, the public has come to expect something new . . . something bold . . . something very action oriented. Their expectations are high. They expect much more than "BS," as you called the original speech.

For any Presidential message to the nation at this time we need to borrow a page from McLuhan.[2] People don't want to hear you *talk* about their problems and they certainly don't want to hear you *whine* about them. They don't want to hear you *talk* about hope and confidence. They don't want to hear you *talk* about leadership. They want to perceive you beginning to *solve* the problems, *inspire* confidence by your actions, and *lead*. You inspire confidence by being *confident*. Leadership begins with a sense of knowing where you're going. The Caddell speech sends all the opposite signals.

No one will even be listening after the first five minutes. But they'll still be receiving signals: uncertainty, petulance, softness. It's an interesting academic treatise. But people want you to do something, to be a President, to be a leader—not to philosophize about it.

I'm afraid that every one of us at Camp David has gotten into the habit of reinforcing one another's ideas. Remember, the audience is going to be tough. It would be nice if everyone thought that the President talked about some interesting and unconventional concepts. More likely, the reaction would be "bullshit." He kept us waiting and watching for ten days to produce this? What's he going to do about the problem?

We must look carefully at each self-deprecating remark and each negative comment about America. We'd hear them thrown back ad nauseam during a campaign, even on the day after the speech. "Jimmy Carter thinks America has lost its spirit. Well, I say he's wrong . . . etc. . . . etc." "After three years in office, Jimmy Carter says that he's failed to lead this country . . . and he's right."

People listen to Presidential speeches the way they listen to rock music. If they heard the same speech a hundred times they still

[2]Marshall McLuhan (1911–1980) was a Canadian writer whose ideas on the nature and power of media had considerable influence in the United States in the 1960s and 1970s.

wouldn't know any of the words. But they "receive" the tone, the beat, the rhythm.

The speech *must* be shorter than 30 minutes. It *must* be action oriented.

The first one-third should recognize the seriousness of the energy problem and the broader concept of the malaise in the country. There should be a short mea culpa by you as the head of government. (This could also be used as analogous to the condition of the country; i.e. "as I have spent so much time presenting programs in my role as head of the government, as opposed to leader of the nation, so have the people in acquiring so many material things and losing our spiritual and ethical and moral values.")

The second third should consist of the 5, 6, or 7 crisp points of your energy program—not detailed, but specific. A series of actions.

The last third of the speech should dwell on America's ability to solve our problems. You should be positive. You should not ramble on about the problems. You should not seem unsure. You should not be negative. People are not turning to Kennedy or Connally[3] because they are attuned to the crisis of confidence in the country but are turning to them because they look like the solution to the crisis.

---

[3]John Connally, former Democratic governor of Texas, was competing with Ronald Reagan for the presidential nomination of the Republican party.

4

Preparation and Delivery
of July 15, 1979, Speech

During the days at Camp David, Carter listened carefully to what he heard—not only from his advisers but also from scores of people from religion, business, labor, politics, and economics. In his diary for July 9, the president noted that it was not easy for him "to accept criticism and to reassess my ways of doing things. And this was a week of intense reassessment."* By July 11, he was ready to draft the speech he would deliver on July 15. Although he relied on his speechwriters, he also played a commanding role in shaping his talk. His handwritten notes reveal both what he absorbed and the differences between raw material and delivered speech. Almost all of the policy initiatives Carter announced on July 15 had been put forward before, but the tone was strikingly more urgent when compared with his previous efforts, most notably his April 18, 1977, address (see Document 1).

*Jimmy Carter, Diary Entry, 9 July 1979, quoted in Jimmy Carter, *Keeping Faith: Memoirs of a President* (New York: Bantam, 1982), 118.

16

JIMMY CARTER

Handwritten Notes in Preparation for Speech

July 11, 1979

These notes, one page of which follows, are what the president culled from his conversations at Camp David as he thought about what he would say. Some of what he wrote down ended up in his speech; some did not. For example, he did not use the following two quotes: "We American Jews have got to do something about the Palestinian refugees" and "With nuclear weapons, we're the first generation to know we may be the last." He also carefully avoided blaming the media for his woes, not using this remark: "We are overly intimidated by a cynical press." Although he did use a modified version of the quote "Our vital organs are stretched over the fence, and our neighbors in OPEC have the knife," he omitted the words of another critic of OPEC who urged, "Millions for defense, but not one cent for tribute."

Tomorrow, in Kansas City, I will present in detail a sound energy program for the Congress and for the people of America. I will not issue BB guns. My proposals will be bold, and we may make some mistakes. I will not let [oil] imports rise between now and 1985, after which the tremendous strength and technology of our nation will drive imports down. Our national security will be protected; our economy can stay strong. Coal, solar, [conservation] and the production of new synthetic fuels will provide the way. This massive national effort to achieve energy security will be expensive, costing [more than] ~~perhaps~~ $100 billion in the next decade. ~~But~~ Unlike payments for foreign oil, these funds will not flow out of our country, but will be paid by Americans to Americans.

Note: Material in brackets indicates words that Carter edited in; strike-throughs indicate words that he deleted.

Jimmy Carter, "Handwritten Notes in Preparation for Speech," 11 July 1979, Office of Staff Secretary: Presidential Handwriting File, box 139, folder "Presidential Address to the Nation, 7/13/79 [2]," JCPL.

Tomorrow, in Kansas City, I will present in detail a sound energy program for the Congress and for the people of America. I will not issue BB guns. My proposals will be bold, and we may make some mistakes. I will not let oil imports rise between now and 1985, after which the tremendous strength and technology of our nation will drive imports down. Our national security will be protected; our economy can stay sharp. Coal, solar, conservation, and the production of new synthetic fuels will provide the way. This massive national effort to achieve energy security will be expensive, costing more than perhaps $100 billion in the next decade. But Unlike payments for foreign oil, these funds will not flow out of our country, but will be paid by Americans to Americans

Jimmy Carter's handwritten notes in preparation for speech, July 11, 1979.

The Daily Diary of President Jimmy Carter
July 15, 1979

Every day, a staff member at the White House composed an official record of what Carter did and to whom he talked. This diary reveals the pace of his activities, the variety of people to whom he talked, and the combination of personal and political tasks on which he focused.

TIME			
FROM	TO	PHONE*	ACTIVITY
6:00		R	The President received a wake up call from the White House signal board operator.
8:41			The President had breakfast with: The First Lady Amy Carter[1]
9:49			The Presidential party went to the South Grounds.
9:51	9:53		The Presidential party motored from the South Grounds to the First Baptist Church, 1328 16th Street.
			The Presidential party was greeted by: Rev. Charles R. Trentham, Pastor of the First Baptist Church Rev. Charles A. Sanks, Jr., Associate Pastor of the First Baptist Church
10:00	10:46		The President and the First Lady attended adult Sunday School class.
10:46	11:58		The President, the First Lady, and Amy Carter attended worship services.
11:59			The Presidential party returned to their motorcade.
11:59	12:02		The Presidential party motored from the First Baptist Church to the South Grounds of the White House.
12:03			The Presidential party returned to the second floor Residence.

*P = Placed; R = Rec'd

[1]Daughter of President and Mrs. Carter.

"The Daily Diary of President Jimmy Carter," 15 July 1979, Presidential Diary Office, box "Presidential Diary 57, 7/15/79," JCPL.

TIME			
FROM	TO	PHONE*	ACTIVITY

FROM	TO	PHONE*	ACTIVITY
12:38		P	The President telephoned his Assistant for Communications, Gerald M. Rafshoon. The call was not completed.
12:42	12:43	R	The President talked with Mr. Rafshoon.
12:45			The President had lunch with: The First Lady Jeff and Annette Carter[2] Mrs. G. C. (Dorothy) Davis, mother of Annette Carter
12:59	1:02	P	The President talked with Chairman of the Council of Economic Advisers (CEA) Charles L. Schultze.
1:34	1:36	P	The President talked with Mr. Rafshoon.
1:43	2:10		The President met with Mr. Rafshoon.
3:32			The President and the First Lady went to the Oval Office.
3:35			The President and the First Lady went to Room 175 in the Old Executive Office Building (OEOB), Mr. Rafshoon's office.
3:35	5:12		The President met with: The First Lady Mr. Rafshoon Patrick J. Caddell, President of Cambridge Survey, Cambridge, Massachusetts (in/out)
4:48		R	The President was telephoned by Senator Bill Bradley (D-New Jersey). The call was not completed.
5:12			The President returned to the Oval Office.
6:09			The President returned to the second floor Residence.
6:13	6:14	P	The President talked with Mr. Rafshoon.
6:26			The President returned to the South Grounds. The President went jogging.
6:45			The President returned to the second floor Residence.
8:54	8:55	R	The President talked with Mr. Rafshoon.
8:55	9:00		The President met with Mr. Rafshoon.
9:34			The President returned to the Oval Office.
9:38	9:39	P	The President talked with Representative Thomas P. O'Neill, Jr. (D-Massachusetts).

*P = Placed; R = Rec'd

[2]Son and daughter-in-law of President and Mrs. Carter.

TIME			
FROM	TO	PHONE*	ACTIVITY
9:40	9:41	P	The President talked with Senator Robert C. Byrd (D-West Virginia).
10:00	10:32		The President addressed the nation on the energy situation. The President's remarks were broadcast live over radio and television.
10:36			The President and the First Lady went to the Roosevelt Room.
10:38?			The President and the First Lady returned to the second floor Residence.
10:38?	10:40	R	The President talked with his son, Jack Carter.
10:41	10:43	P	The President talked with his mother, Mrs. Lillian Carter.
10:53		R	The President was telephoned by Mr. Caddell. The call was not completed.
10:54	10:55	R	The President talked with Vice President Walter F. Mondale.
10:55	11:00	P	The President talked with Mr. Caddell.
11:21	11:22	R	The President talked with Representative O'Neill.
11:45			The President retired.
11:53		P	The President gave a message to the White House signal board operator.

*P = Placed; R = Rec'd

18

JIMMY CARTER

Energy and National Goals

July 15, 1979

This speech, the most important of Carter's presidency, was known by various names, including "Energy and the Crisis of Confidence" and the "malaise speech." Compared with the one he delivered on April 18, 1977 (see Document 1), it was more morally charged. It also revealed how

Jimmy Carter, "Energy and National Goals," 15 July 1979, *Public Papers of the Presidents of the United States: Jimmy Carter, 1977–81* (Washington, D.C.: Government Printing Office, 1979), 2:1235–41.

Carter solved the problems posed by the widely contradictory advice he received.

Good evening.
This is a special night for me. Exactly 3 years ago, on July 15, 1976, I accepted the nomination of my party to run for President of the United States. I promised you a President who is not isolated from the people, who feels your pain, and who shares your dreams and who draws his strength and his wisdom from you.

During the past 3 years I've spoken to you on many occasions about national concerns, the energy crisis, reorganizing the Government, our Nation's economy, and issues of war and especially peace. But over those years the subjects of the speeches, the talks, and the press conferences have become increasingly narrow, focused more and more on what the isolated world of Washington thinks is important. Gradually, you've heard more and more about what the Government thinks or what the Government should be doing and less and less about our Nation's hopes, our dreams, and our vision of the future.

Ten days ago I had planned to speak to you again about a very important subject—energy. For the fifth time I would have described the urgency of the problem and laid out a series of legislative recommendations to the Congress. But as I was preparing to speak, I began to ask myself the same question that I now know has been troubling many of you. Why have we not been able to get together as a nation to resolve our serious energy problem?

It's clear that the true problems of our Nation are much deeper— deeper than gasoline lines or energy shortages, deeper even than inflation or recession. And I realize more than ever that as President I need your help. So, I decided to reach out and listen to the voices of America.

I invited to Camp David people from almost every segment of our society—business and labor, teachers and preachers, governors, mayors, and private citizens. And then I left Camp David to listen to other Americans, men and women like you. It has been an extraordinary 10 days, and I want to share with you what I've heard.

First of all, I got a lot of personal advice. Let me quote a few of the typical comments that I wrote down.

This from a southern Governor: "Mr. President, you are not leading this Nation—you're just managing the Government."

"You don't see the people enough any more."

"Some of your Cabinet members don't seem loyal. There is not enough discipline among your disciples."

"Don't talk to us about politics or the mechanics of government, but about an understanding of our common good."

"Mr. President, we're in trouble. Talk to us about blood and sweat and tears."

"If you lead, Mr. President, we will follow."

Many people talked about themselves and about the condition of our Nation. This from a young woman in Pennsylvania: "I feel so far from government. I feel like ordinary people are excluded from political power."

And this from a young Chicano: "Some of us have suffered from recession all our lives."

"Some people have wasted energy, but others haven't had anything to waste."

And this from a religious leader: "No material shortage can touch the important things like God's love for us or our love for one another."

And I like this one particularly from a black woman who happens to be the mayor of a small Mississippi town: "The big-shots are not the only ones who are important. Remember, you can't sell anything on Wall Street unless someone digs it up somewhere else first."

This kind of summarized a lot of other statements: "Mr. President, we are confronted with a moral and a spiritual crisis."

Several of our discussions were on energy, and I have a notebook full of comments and advice. I'll read just a few.

"We can't go on consuming 40 percent more energy than we produce. When we import oil we are also importing inflation plus unemployment."

"We've got to use what we have. The Middle East has only 5 percent of the world's energy, but the United States has 24 percent."

And this is one of the most vivid statements: "Our neck is stretched over the fence and OPEC has a knife."

"There will be other cartels and other shortages. American wisdom and courage right now can set a path to follow in the future."

This was a good one: "Be bold, Mr. President. We may make mistakes, but we are ready to experiment."

And this one from a labor leader got to the heart of it: "The real issue is freedom. We must deal with the energy problem on a war footing."

And the last that I'll read: "When we enter the moral equivalent of war, Mr. President, don't issue us BB guns."

These 10 days confirmed my belief in the decency and the strength and the wisdom of the American people, but it also bore out some of my long-standing concerns about our Nation's underlying problems.

I know, of course, being President, that government actions and legislation can be very important. That's why I've worked hard to put my campaign promises into law—and I have to admit, with just mixed success. But after listening to the American people I have been reminded again that all the legislation in the world can't fix what's wrong with America. So, I want to speak to you first tonight about a subject even more serious than energy or inflation. I want to talk to you right now about a fundamental threat to American democracy.

I do not mean our political and civil liberties. They will endure. And I do not refer to the outward strength of America, a nation that is at peace tonight everywhere in the world, with unmatched economic power and military might.

The threat is nearly invisible in ordinary ways. It is a crisis of confidence. It is a crisis that strikes at the very heart and soul and spirit of our national will. We can see this crisis in the growing doubt about the meaning of our own lives and in the loss of a unity of purpose for our Nation.

The erosion of our confidence in the future is threatening to destroy the social and the political fabric of America.

The confidence that we have always had as a people is not simply some romantic dream or a proverb in a dusty book that we read just on the Fourth of July. It is the idea which founded our Nation and has guided our development as a people. Confidence in the future has supported everything else—public institutions and private enterprise, our own families, and the very Constitution of the United States. Confidence has defined our course and has served as a link between generations. We've always believed in something called progress. We've always had a faith that the days of our children would be better than our own.

Our people are losing that faith, not only in government itself but in the ability as citizens to serve as the ultimate rulers and shapers of our democracy. As a people we know our past and we are proud of it. Our progress has been part of the living history of America, even the world. We always believed that we were part of a great movement of humanity itself called democracy, involved in the search for freedom,

and that belief has always strengthened us in our purpose. But just as we are losing our confidence in the future, we are also beginning to close the door on our past.

In a nation that was proud of hard work, strong families, close-knit communities, and our faith in God, too many of us now tend to worship self-indulgence and consumption. Human identity is no longer defined by what one does, but by what one owns. But we've discovered that owning things and consuming things does not satisfy our longing for meaning. We've learned that piling up material goods cannot fill the emptiness of lives which have no confidence or purpose.

The symptoms of this crisis of the American spirit are all around us. For the first time in the history of our country a majority of our people believe that the next 5 years will be worse than the past 5 years. Two-thirds of our people do not even vote. The productivity of American workers is actually dropping, and the willingness of Americans to save for the future has fallen below that of all other people in the Western world.

As you know, there is a growing disrespect for government and for churches and for schools, the news media, and other institutions. This is not a message of happiness or reassurance, but it is the truth and it is a warning.

These changes did not happen overnight. They've come upon us gradually over the last generation, years that were filled with shocks and tragedy.

We were sure that ours was a nation of the ballot, not the bullet, until the murders of John Kennedy and Robert Kennedy and Martin Luther King, Jr. We were taught that our armies were always invincible and our causes always just, only to suffer the agony of Vietnam. We respected the Presidency as a place of honor until the shock of Watergate.

We remember when the phrase "sound as a dollar" was an expression of absolute dependability, until 10 years of inflation began to shrink our dollar and our savings. We believed that our Nation's resources were limitless until 1973, when we had to face a growing dependence on foreign oil.

These wounds are still very deep. They have never been healed.

Opposite: Toward the end of the Camp David energy meeting, on July 13, 1979, President Carter and his advisers made a visit to the home of Mr. and Mrs. Martin Porterfield in Martinsburg, West Virginia. On the president's left is Rosalynn Carter and next to her is Patrick Caddell.

Presidential photographs, #11920 by Schumacher, JCPL.

Looking for a way out of this crisis, our people have turned to the Federal Government and found it isolated from the mainstream of our Nation's life. Washington, D.C., has become an island. The gap between our citizens and our Government has never been so wide. The people are looking for honest answers, not easy answers; clear leadership, not false claims and evasiveness and politics as usual.

What you see too often in Washington and elsewhere around the country is a system of government that seems incapable of action. You see a Congress twisted and pulled in every direction by hundreds of well-financed and powerful special interests. You see every extreme position defended to the last vote, almost to the last breath by one unyielding group or another. You often see a balanced and a fair approach that demands sacrifice, a little sacrifice from everyone, abandoned like an orphan without support and without friends.

Often you see paralysis and stagnation and drift. You don't like it, and neither do I. What can we do?

First of all, we must face the truth, and then we can change our course. We simply must have faith in each other, faith in our ability to govern ourselves, and faith in the future of this Nation. Restoring that faith and that confidence to America is now the most important task we face. It is a true challenge of this generation of Americans.

One of the visitors to Camp David last week put it this way: "We've got to stop crying and start sweating, stop talking and start walking, stop cursing and start praying. The strength we need will not come from the White House, but from every house in America."

We know the strength of America. We are strong. We can regain our unity. We can regain our confidence. We are the heirs of generations who survived threats much more powerful and awesome than those that challenge us now. Our fathers and mothers were strong men and women who shaped a new society during the Great Depression, who fought world wars, and who carved out a new charter of peace for the world.

We ourselves are the same Americans who just 10 years ago put a man on the Moon. We are the generation that dedicated our society to the pursuit of human rights and equality. And we are the generation that will win the war on the energy problem and in that process rebuild the unity and confidence of America.

We are at a turning point in our history. There are two paths to choose. One is a path I've warned about tonight, the path that leads to fragmentation and self-interest. Down that road lies a mistaken idea of freedom, the right to grasp for ourselves some advantage over others. That path would be one of constant conflict between narrow interests ending in chaos and immobility. It is a certain route to failure.

All the traditions of our past, all the lessons of our heritage, all the promises of our future point to another path, the path of common purpose and the restoration of American values. That path leads to true freedom for our Nation and ourselves. We can take the first steps down that path as we begin to solve our energy problem.

Energy will be the immediate test of our ability to unite this Nation, and it can also be the standard around which we rally. On the battlefield of energy we can win for our Nation a new confidence, and we can seize control again of our common destiny.

In little more than two decades we've gone from a position of energy independence to one in which almost half the oil we use comes from foreign countries, at prices that are going through the roof. Our excessive dependence on OPEC has already taken a tremendous toll on our economy and our people. This is the direct cause of the long lines which have made millions of you spend aggravating hours waiting for gasoline. It's a cause of the increased inflation and unemployment that we now face. This intolerable dependence on foreign oil threatens our economic independence and the very security of our Nation.

The energy crisis is real. It is worldwide. It is a clear and present danger to our Nation. These are facts and we simply must face them.

What I have to say to you now about energy is simple and vitally important.

Point one: I am tonight setting a clear goal for the energy policy of the United States. Beginning this moment, this Nation will never use more foreign oil than we did in 1977—never. From now on, every new addition to our demand for energy will be met from our own production and our own conservation. The generation-long growth in our dependence on foreign oil will be stopped dead in its tracks right now and then reversed as we move through the 1980s, for I am tonight setting the further goal of cutting our dependence on foreign oil by one-half by the end of the next decade—a saving of over 4½ million barrels of imported oil per day.

Point two: To ensure that we meet these targets, I will use my Presidential authority to set import quotas. I'm announcing tonight that for 1979 and 1980, I will forbid the entry into this country of one drop of foreign oil more than these goals allow. These quotas will ensure a reduction in imports even below the ambitious levels we set at the recent Tokyo summit.

Point three: To give us energy security, I am asking for the most massive peacetime commitment of funds and resources in our Nation's history to develop America's own alternative sources of fuel— from coal, from oil shale, from plant products for gasohol, from unconventional gas, from the Sun.

I propose the creation of an energy security corporation to lead this effort to replace 2½ million barrels of imported oil per day by 1990. The corporation will issue up to $5 billion in energy bonds, and I especially want them to be in small denominations so that average Americans can invest directly in America's energy security.

Just as a similar synthetic rubber corporation helped us win World War II, so will we mobilize American determination and ability to win the energy war. Moreover, I will soon submit legislation to Congress calling for the creation of this Nation's first solar bank, which will help us achieve the crucial goal of 20 percent of our energy coming from solar power by the year 2000.

These efforts will cost money, a lot of money, and that is why Congress must enact the windfall profits tax without delay. It will be money well spent. Unlike the billions of dollars that we ship to foreign countries to pay for foreign oil, these funds will be paid by Americans to Americans. These funds will go to fight, not to increase, inflation and unemployment.

Point four: I'm asking Congress to mandate, to require as a matter of law, that our Nation's utility companies cut their massive use of oil by 50 percent within the next decade and switch to other fuels, especially coal, our most abundant energy source.

Point five: To make absolutely certain that nothing stands in the way of achieving these goals, I will urge Congress to create an energy mobilization board which, like the War Production Board in World War II, will have the responsibility and authority to cut through the red tape, the delays, and the endless roadblocks to completing key energy projects.

We will protect our environment. But when this Nation critically needs a refinery or a pipeline, we will build it.

Point six: I'm proposing a bold conservation program to involve every State, county, and city and every average American in our energy battle. This effort will permit you to build conservation into your homes and your lives at a cost you can afford.

I ask Congress to give me authority for mandatory conservation and for standby gasoline rationing. To further conserve energy, I'm proposing tonight an extra $10 billion over the next decade to strengthen our public transportation systems. And I'm asking you for your good and for your Nation's security to take no unnecessary trips, to use carpools or public transportation whenever you can, to park your car one extra day per week, to obey the speed limit, and to set your thermostats to save fuel. Every act of energy conservation like this is more than just common sense—I tell you it is an act of patriotism.

Our Nation must be fair to the poorest among us, so we will increase aid to needy Americans to cope with rising energy prices. We often think of conservation only in terms of sacrifice. In fact, it is the most painless and immediate way of rebuilding our Nation's strength. Every gallon of oil each one of us saves is a new form of production. It gives us more freedom, more confidence, that much more control over our own lives.

So, the solution of our energy crisis can also help us to conquer the crisis of the spirit in our country. It can rekindle our sense of unity, our confidence in the future, and give our Nation and all of us individually a new sense of purpose.

You know we can do it. We have the natural resources. We have more oil in our shale alone than several Saudi Arabias. We have more coal than any nation on Earth. We have the world's highest level of technology. We have the most skilled work force, with innovative genius, and I firmly believe that we have the national will to win this war.

I do not promise you that this struggle for freedom will be easy. I do not promise a quick way out of our Nation's problems, when the truth is that the only way out is an all-out effort. What I do promise you is that I will lead our fight, and I will enforce fairness in our struggle, and I will ensure honesty. And above all, I will act.

We can manage the short-term shortages more effectively and we will, but there are no short-term solutions to our long-range problems. There is simply no way to avoid sacrifice.

Twelve hours from now I will speak again in Kansas City, to expand and to explain further our energy program. Just as the search for solutions to our energy shortages has now led us to a new awareness of our Nation's deeper problems, so our willingness to work for those solutions in energy can strengthen us to attack those deeper problems.

I will continue to travel this country, to hear the people of America. You can help me to develop a national agenda for the 1980s. I will lis-

President Carter delivering the "crisis of confidence" speech, July 15, 1979. Presidential photographs, #11942 by Fackelman, JCPL.

ten and I will act. We will act together. These were the promises I made 3 years ago, and I intend to keep them.

Little by little we can and we must rebuild our confidence. We can spend until we empty our treasuries, and we may summon all the wonders of science. But we can succeed only if we tap our greatest resources—America's people, America's values, and America's confidence.

I have seen the strength of America in the inexhaustible resources of our people. In the days to come, let us renew that strength in the struggle for an energy-secure nation.

In closing, let me say this: I will do my best, but I will not do it alone. Let your voice be heard. Whenever you have a chance, say something good about our country. With God's help and for the sake of our Nation, it is time for us to join hands in America. Let us commit ourselves together to a rebirth of the American spirit. Working together with our common faith we cannot fail.

Thank you and good night.

5

Reactions to the Speech

The documents in this chapter suggest both the intensity and the variety of the reactions to Carter's "crisis of confidence" speech. The speech itself, with its distinct sections, was sufficiently complex so that people with varied political, personal, and moral perspectives could interpret it in different ways. The brief period between July 15 and the president's ill-advised reshuffling of his cabinet several days later provided an interlude when he and his supporters basked in the light of dramatically improved ratings in the polls.

THE PRESS

Every day except Sunday, the staff in the White House prepares a summary of national and international news so that members of the administration, including the president, can have convenient access to how the media are covering presidential decisions. The White House news summaries* of July 17 and 18, 1979, captured the response of the media. Columnists weighed in with their assessments. Don Campbell of the Gannett News Service hailed Carter's efforts as "the most forceful speech Carter has made as president." In the *New York Daily News,* James Wieghart disagreed, asserting that only one problem remained for the president to solve: "how to wake up the 80 million Americans Carter put to sleep last night." Editorials offered varied assessments. One in the *Los Angeles Times* was typical in its two-sided approach. On the one hand, the editorial chided the president for "scolding his fellow citizens" like "a pastor with a profligate flock." On the other hand, it welcomed the effort to join "in what Carter called a common purpose of crucial importance to an entire generation" as

---

*These quotes are from "The White House News Summary," 17 and 18 July 1979, Daily White House News, JCPL.

a first step in restoring "the nation's confidence in its government, its President, its churches and its other institutions." The *Baltimore Sun* was more unalloyed in its praise, applauding Carter's "new determination, his new boldness," qualities not seen since he entered the White House.

Conservatives

19

THE WALL STREET JOURNAL

The Real Jimmy Carter: Editorial

July 17, 1979

This editorial appeared in the The Wall Street Journal, *the nation's most widely read business newspaper. It captured the response of many leaders in the corporate world, who were skeptical of Carter's jeremiad and critical of his reliance on big government, rather than free markets, to solve the energy problems.*

Out of all the sermonic and confusing rhetoric President Carter has showered on the American public these last two days, at least one thing is clear. The President has weighed the merits of either getting the government out of the energy business or getting it more deeply in. He has chosen to get it further in, on a massive, almost unbelievable scale. The real Jimmy Carter has finally stood up, and on the far left of the Democratic Party.

There'll be a new government "Energy Security Corp." to siphon $140 billion in "windfall profits" from the oil companies over the next 10 years. That would pretty much eliminate oil profits of any kind. While the oil companies quietly pass out of business, the ESC would squander this money on expensive and technologically risky forms of energy.

There'll be an Energy Mobilization Board to ride roughshod over

Editorial, "The Real Jimmy Carter," *The Wall Street Journal,* 17 July 1979, 18.

normal legal processes, except maybe those that are mainly responsible for retarding energy development, the environmental laws, for example.

There'll be a new army of government inspectors scouring the country, levying $10,000 fines on any hapless building operator whose thermostats are showing something less than 78 degrees. Electric utilities will be "made" to switch out of oil—as if they themselves, and not the government, are to blame for their not doing that.

There'll be a federal "Solar Bank" finally to capture the elusive riches of solar power. The President will set conservative goals for states, import quotas for the nation, etc.

In short, Mr. Carter has reacted to the public's low opinion of his administration by "getting tough" and proposing a further suspension of private freedoms. He justifies this on grounds that it is the American people, not his administration and the Congress, who deserve the blame for our economic problems. He summons up the memory of Franklin Roosevelt as he casts himself in the role of a President leading the country out of an awful crisis; except where FDR confronted Depression and poverty, Mr. Carter seems to find his crisis in excessive affluence:

"Too many of us now tend to worship self-indulgence and consumption . . . we have learned that piling up material goods cannot fill the emptiness of lives which have no confidence or purpose . . . the symptoms of this crisis of the American spirit are all around us: two-thirds of our people do not even vote, the productivity of American workers is actually dropping and the willingness of Americans to save for the future has fallen below that of all other people in the Western world . . . there is a growing disrespect for government and for churches and schools, the news media, and other institutions. . . ."

Quite an indictment. It is the kind of indictment clergymen use to lash their congregations with on Sunday mornings and it is appropriate in that setting of spiritual redemption. But it is highly inappropriate coming from the man who is supposed to be managing the affairs of the United States government. The two key problems that provoked this rhetorical outburst—inflation and gasoline lines—are clearly and directly attributable to the policies of the Carter administration.

The gasoline lines are caused by the government's refusal to remove price controls, and hence supply allocations. Given the enormous economic inefficiencies that have resulted from this refusal, it now seems clear that prices of gasoline would fall, not rise further, after decontrol. Other forms of government intervention—energy use regulation and draconian environmental rules, in particular—have added to the dislocations and inefficiencies. It doesn't take a $140 billion government program to solve an energy problem; the problem would evaporate if the government would simply get out of energy.

As to those other problems of the American "spirit," low savings and productivity and low confidence in institutions—the main cause is inflation. Why should anyone have confidence in a government that can't balance its budget and run a stable monetary policy? Or why should they save the money it prints?

Now, it seems, it will be necessary to print still more money, and generate still more inflation, to finance the latest grandiose schemes dreamed up by the statists who hold the President in their grip. They are in the saddle and they are exultant about the President's vigorous showmanship Sunday night and Monday. The only trouble is that the policies he has proposed will only get the country into a deeper tangle. And next year, the voters will have a chance to decide which side *they're* on—or at least so we hope.

20

NATIONAL REVIEW

Gantry on Energy: Editorial

August 3, 1979

The title of this editorial column in the National Review, *the nation's most influential conservative weekly, refers to the main figure in Sinclair Lewis's novel* Elmer Gantry *(1927), about an evangelical preacher whose actions contradicted his beliefs. The author, perhaps the magazine's founder, William F. Buckley Jr., offered a head-on critique of the president's assertion that what plagued America was a spiritual crisis caused by affluence and the pursuit of self-realization through material possessions. The quotations from Republican presidential hopeful John Connally reflected the belief of conservatives that the solution to the nation's energy problem was not government intervention but the operation of free markets.*

Editorial, "Gantry on Energy," *National Review,* 3 Aug. 1979, 953–56.

1. Style

Beginning with Jimmy Carter's first appearance on the national scene, it has always been necessary to separate style from substance. But nothing even remotely like his July 15 televised address to the nation occurs to us.

Carter prepared for this media event by doing a Moses number. He withdrew to the Mountain. He then gathered the Tribes around him, all the energy experts, like Jesse Jackson and Lane Kirkland, Bob Keefe and Mayor Koch, John Kenneth Galbraith and Clark Clifford.[1] The guest list, it is written, was compiled by the Great Rafshoon. Then Moses descended, and went on TV.

First of all, the visual impression. It was the Resurrection number. For the first twenty minutes or so, the leader of the free world seemed close to tears. He flagellated himself rhetorically, quoting pungent criticisms of his performance as President. But surely, one supposed, something was going to happen, some Third Birth,[2] some abortion, *something.* . . .

Midway through this extraordinary performance, Carter made his play. He sought to deflect attention to our "real" problem, which surprisingly enough doesn't have much to do with such things as gasoline lines, inflation, government roadblocks, reverse discrimination, our triumphs in Rhodesia, Taiwan, and Indochina.

Our *real* problem isn't energy. It's eschatology![3]

In this amazing discourse our problems are not plain and manifest but "underlying," a "crisis that strikes at the very heart and soul and spirit of our nation," a "crisis in the growing doubt about the meaning of our own lives and in the loss of a unity of purpose for our nation." "We have learned that piling up material goods cannot fill the emptiness of lives which have no confidence or purpose."

The U.S. Government has nothing to do with spiritual crises or the meaning of our lives, and had best leave that sort of thing to Dante, T. S. Eliot, and individual reflection. The last time we looked, God was not a member of the Carter Cabinet.

People want the U.S. Government to do a few practical things it is

---

[1] Lane Kirkland was president of the AFL-CIO from 1979 to 1995; Robert Keefe was a Washington political consultant; Clark Clifford, a Washington lawyer, advised Democratic presidents from Harry S. Truman to Bill Clinton.

[2] A spiritual transformation, following the physical first birth and the second one at baptism.

[3] A field within theology that is concerned with ultimate issues such as death or the end of the universe.

competent to do. It would not have hurt a bit if the U.S. Government had been able to defeat a minor aggressor in Southeast Asia. It would certainly help right now if the U.S. Government could get out the way of a gallon of gas.

Amidst all this obfuscation and Elmer Gantryism—it would in fact be unkind to believe in Carter's sincerity—we treasure the following sentence from his speech as an absolute collector's item: "As you know there is a growing disrespect for government and for churches and for schools, the news media, and other institutions."

The news media! Just imagine that. Disrespect for *the news media.* Who would've thunk it. What a symptom of moral decline. And look more closely. Is there really increasing disrespect for *churches?* for *schools* (as distinguished from legitimate criticism)? We doubt it.

But no doubt we are wrong. As Carter used to say, "I'll never lie to you."

2. Program Notes

President Carter believes the U.S. has an energy problem because (1) Americans waste energy, and (2) the U.S. is too dependent on energy imports, thus endangering the dollar and the independence of our foreign policy. The solution he proposes has three main features: mandatory conservation to stop U.S. energy imports from growing, a domestic synthetic fuel program to permit a reduction in future imports, and a new $24-billion transfer program to help the poor pay their energy bills.

The conservation policies consist of quotas holding oil imports to their 1977 level, mandatory temperature restrictions at work places, and standby gasoline rationing. The President already has the first two powers and ordered the policies into effect. For gasoline rationing, synthetic fuels, and "energy stamps," he needs congressional cooperation.

The President envisions an Energy Security Corporation funded with $88 billion in "windfall profits taxes" on domestic oil producers. This new government enterprise will have vast powers to go with its vast sums. It will decide without considering profitability or price how to invest a sizable chunk of the nation's capital.

The form in which the President's proposals will emerge from Congress is unclear. The $88-billion synfuel program may turn out to be too big a boondoggle for the Congress to digest. Divvying up such a large program between congressional districts and the various interests takes time. Each political player has an incentive to withhold agreement in hopes of obtaining a larger share. Something like this happened earlier to the "windfall profits tax" when Congress couldn't agree how to spend the revenues it would raise.

Nevertheless, the economic and political implications of the President's program are worthy of more comment than they have received. Looking first at the conservation measures, in imposing oil quotas the President has eliminated an important safety valve. The next time snafus develop in federal energy allocations, the government can't turn to the international market for supplies. This could be more serious than gasoline lines or home-heating-oil shortages. Right now the economy is beginning to slacken, so the quota is not a constraint. But when the economy begins another expansion the quota is likely to abort it for lack of fuel. Conservation is not free; it costs jobs and production.

The temperature restrictions will add sweltering and shivering to the annoyances of the work place, and the value of the production lost from the added stress will exceed the energy "saved." There will be political costs as well, because people's idealism will soon dissolve into discomfort, and they will hold the President responsible. Gasoline rationing is guaranteed to be a political nightmare. If the bureaucrats can't get gasoline allocations right among fifty states, they can't cope with allocations to 110 million motorists. And the price controls are prompting political organization among service station operators and the threat of strikes, thus extending organized unrest into a new sector of the economy.

The synfuel program is much more costly to the economy than even $88 billion suggests. Consider for example the lost production of lower-priced natural energy that is a consequence of diverting oil company revenues to the production of higher-priced government synfuel. Or the cost overruns that will accompany the transformation of the energy industry into government contractors. To put the $88 billion in perspective, in 1978 total expenditures for plant and equipment by the manufacturing sector came to less than $68 billion.

It is a foregone conclusion that any synthetic fuel that results from the massive diversion of the nation's investment capital will be more costly than the OPEC oil it replaces. This puts the oil import quota in a new light. Properly seen, it is a tariff to protect the government's high-cost synfuel from being undersold on the world market.

The President's program would saddle the nation with massive resource commitments that would leave future Presidents with little leeway to shore up Social Security, defense, or the capital stock on which the economy's growth and our standard of living depend.

3. "If I Were President . . ."

In a bit of enterprising journalism, the *New York Post* asked presidential contender John Connally what he would have said to the people on TV had he been President. Connally was not shy. A few excerpts:

"If I had been the President speaking Sunday night, I first of all would have explained to the American people just how we got in this shape on energy.

"I would have pointed out that the dilemma in which we find ourselves is not the result of any 'malaise of the spirit' of our people. It is rather the inevitable consequence of unwise public policies which we have pursued in this country for many years. It's the politicians who are largely to blame, not the people. . . .

"We made one of our most serious mistakes as a nation when the Federal Power Commission in 1954 decreed an unrealistic ceiling on the price of natural gas at the well-head, despite the pleading of well-informed authorities. What this did was to create an artificially low price for gas and thus encourage its use in unwise and wasteful applications. By so doing, we rapidly accelerated the consumption of natural gas and made the use of coal uneconomical, undercutting and almost destroying the coal industry. . . .

"While I fully support the all-out development of solar, geothermal, and every other kind of potential or synthetic energy source, we will be dependent on oil and gas, coal and nuclear energy for the rest of this century whether we like it or not. My top priority would be to seek congressional authority to relax environmental standards to permit the mining and burning of more coal in this country. I would urge all electric utilities to burn coal wherever possible.

"I would immediately deregulate all oil and gas to encourage every possible exploration for new hydrocarbon reserves in the country, to reverse the current trend of 3.5 per cent loss in production. This could be done today with the stroke of a presidential pen. And in support of that move, I would open up new publicly owned lands both onshore and offshore for that exploration.

"I would urge Congress to get rid of red tape and regulations which now make it impossible to build a nuclear power plant in less than 13 years when the rest of the world does it in 6.5 years. At the same time, I would insist on more rigorous plant inspections to ensure maximum public safeguards. We should renew research on the fast-breeder reactor, focus on reprocessing of spent fuel, and strive to regain leadership in the field which we pioneered. . . .

"It is imperative that we make gasoline out of coal and gas out of coal. . . .

"Finally, and of great significance, I would attempt to arrange an immediate meeting with the newly elected Prime Minister of Canada and the President of Mexico to explore the establishment of a North American Common Market for energy. The combined resources of our three nations, both natural and technological, are of awesome magnitude if developed in harmony on a fully equal basis.

"Beyond the subject of energy, I would stress to the American people that our energy crisis is a current example of the failure of political solutions to solve economic problems.

"Finally, I would tell Americans that there is nothing wrong with the spirit of our people that strong, forceful decisive leadership won't cure. . . ."

And we say that's Secretariat versus the milkman's horse.

4. Resignation Time

President Carter's staff and Cabinet have submitted their resignations, in a move meant to display Decisive Leadership on the part of Carter. He's now in charge, we're meant to understand, and no kidding. The move had eerie overtones. At his first Cabinet meeting after his 1972 landslide, Richard Nixon sat there sourly while Bob Haldeman requested everyone's resignation. It was a brutal and uncalled-for way to assert authority.

In Carter's case, who really cares? Can you, quick, name the Secretary of Labor? Of the Treasury? This must be the most lackluster crew ever assembled in the West Wing of the White House. Word has been leaked that the resignations of the foreign policy team will not be accepted, no doubt in view of their brilliant performance. Andrew Young's position is secure, aargh. To use an electrical metaphor, if you eliminate all the negative charges, you gradually work your way back to zero, and that would be a relief.

Come to think of it, why don't *they* ask for *his* resignation?

Left

21

PROGRESSIVE

Carter's Crisis—and Ours: Comment

September 1979

This response from the Progressive, *a respected left-wing magazine published in Madison, Wisconsin, made clear that although conservatives believed that Carter's commitment to coordinated government action placed him on the left wing of the Democratic party, many of the left took issue with his approach. The editors suggested that neither the president nor the nation wished to address the economic and political problems that the energy crisis revealed.*

President Carter's peculiar performance in July—his abrupt cancellation of his major energy speech, his ten days of mysterious mountaintop musings, his purge of the Cabinet and White House staff—left Americans perplexed and foreigners befuddled. The dollar sank again on overseas markets, and the price of gold reached new heights. Members of Congress took to the floor to speculate aloud about the President's mental health. His popularity, as measured by the public opinion polls, recovered slightly after his delayed energy speech, but then took another dive. The image was of an Administration in acute disarray—and for once the image seemed to correspond to the reality.

The "crisis of confidence" to which Carter repeatedly made reference was genuine enough—but its essence was not, as he implied, that Americans had lost confidence in themselves, but that they had lost confidence in him and his Administration. And it seemed likely that Carter himself shared that loss of confidence.

What Jimmy Carter discovered, a little more than halfway through his four-year term, was that *he had no answers* for the intractable problems confronting this nation and the world. The qualities that brought

"Carter's Crisis—and Ours," *Progressive,* Sept. 1979, 6–8.

him to the White House—the country-boy smile, the reborn Christianity, the common sense of an "outsider" who would straighten out the mess created by the "insiders," the pragmatism of a former Navy officer and engineer (*Why Not the Best?*)[1]—turned out to be irrelevant when it came to coping with an arms race out of control, an energy crisis beyond quick-fix repair, and an economy in precipitate decline.

The blame lies less with Carter than with us: We elected him for those irrelevant qualities and we continue to tolerate (though fewer and fewer of us take an active part in) a system of irrelevant politics. Confronted with a political and economic structure that simply cannot work, we still put our trust in "leaders" whose commitment is to preserving that structure rather than abandoning it.

When Carter campaigned for the Presidency, he had no difficulty identifying the issues that troubled Americans. He called for reduced military spending (without addressing the essential nature of the warfare state). He called for environmental safeguards (without examining the corporate momentum to pollute for the sake of profit). He called for reduced inflation and a return to full employment (without recognizing the dynamic that drives our irrational economy). In these circumstances, it was inevitable that his promises would be betrayed. Bound by the limitations of the status quo, this President—any President—can only fail.

Carter's energy program, produced by the high drama of his retreat to Camp David, is a case in point. The mountain labored and brought forth a mouse.

The centerpiece of the Carter energy program is a commitment to the massive development of synthetic fuels from coal and oil shale. The instrument for this is to be an Energy Security Corporation financed by revenue from the windfall profits tax. The cost is not yet clear, but preliminary estimates suggest that at least $100 billion in Federal funds would be needed to produce 2.5 million barrels a day by 1990. The gasoline obtained in this fashion will be extremely expensive: A small-scale project in South Africa, the only nation presently using this technology, produces gas at about $2.70 a gallon from coal mined at one-third the cost of U.S. coal and processed without the burdens of environmental protection safeguards.

Oil company taxes would pay for the project initially, but the industry would derive long-range benefits far in excess of its contribution.

[1]The title of a 1975 book by Jimmy Carter.

Oil companies already own about half of U.S. coal reserves, and the biggest firms have a substantial foothold in the new synthetic fuel technology. Exxon, for example, has a $240 million pilot project for converting coal to liquid fuel. Hill Bonin, a Gulf Oil lobbyist, has predicted that Federal "front-end money" will assure a prominent oil industry role in synthetic fuel development because project failure would no longer mean "you've got a $1-to-$2 billion white elephant on your hands." As with nuclear power, the U.S. taxpayer would bear the risks and large corporations would reap the profits.

Carter is not the first to suggest private subsidies for development of synthetic fuels. Former Vice President Nelson Rockefeller proposed a $100 billion U.S. energy corporation which would have committed substantial capital to such projects. Earlier proposals for synthetic fuel development have been heavily criticized on the grounds that severe environmental risks would be incurred for a costly and improbable return. A two-million-barrel-a-day shale oil industry would require the equivalent of digging and refilling the Panama Canal every day. Vastly expanded mining and burning of coal would cause widespread acid rains, which kill fish and wildlife, and lead to possible climatic changes through the buildup of carbon dioxide in the atmosphere.

Yet Carter is incapable of recognizing these impediments. He has called for an Energy Mobilization Board to "cut red tape" and speed the development of energy projects. The board would have the right to designate certain projects as critical to the nation and to set strict deadlines for the issuance of Federal, state, and local construction permits. The board could waive requirements for environmental impact statements and public hearings.

And the President has made clear the Administration's continuing determination to push nuclear power regardless of political obstacles: "Nuclear energy must play an important role in the United States to ensure our energy future."

The Energy Mobilization Board, coupled with the Nuclear Siting Bill still being pushed by the Administration, would give the Federal Government vast powers to push energy projects. These measures would effectively deprive citizens of the opportunity to participate in energy decisions. For almost thirty years the Atomic Energy Commission enjoyed such a monopoly of power and information—and the public is still paying the environmental, financial, and political costs.

Carter's "solution" will neither solve the present energy crisis nor restore the nation's confidence. Americans have shown they are willing to change their lifestyle and endure sacrifices if they have the facts and are given some realistic alternatives. In those few areas of the country where trains are available, ridership has increased dramatically. Use of the Los Angeles-to-San Diego line has exceeded World War II records, and bookings for Amtrak are up 90 per cent over last year. Giving citizens the information and the resources they need to plan local and regional transportation policy is the best way to lessen their dependence on the automobile.

Similarly, a long-range solution to the energy crisis will require more public participation in a wide range of decisions about energy production and utilization, such as the drain on energy and oil represented by such corporate guzzlers as the plastics and aluminum industries. James Ridgeway reports in a new book, *Energy-Efficient Community Planning,* that some local communities are now beginning rudimentary efforts to plan transportation, land use, and farming patterns to maximize energy resources. Programs have included use of vacant lots for urban farming and continuous energy audits of local buildings to reduce fuel consumption.

But the Carter program will provide neither the resources nor the opportunity for the comprehensive national and local planning needed if we are to achieve a secure and safe energy future. The most important decisions and information will be out of our hands. And despite comforting rhetoric about a solar future, the massive open-ended commitment to nuclear and synthetic fuel will leave little capital for safer, more effective alternatives. The Carter program is not a prescription for conservation or renewable energy sources; it will conserve only the power of established corporate elites.

That same priority governs the Carter approach to our economic crisis. Administration economists have now confirmed what a number of private economists were saying for months: The U.S. economy is heading into a severe recession in the last half of this year. Gross national product will decline, lagging economic growth will push the official rate of unemployment up another full percentage point, and the annual inflation rate will reach 10.4 per cent. Some Administration economists believe even these projections are optimistic and could be worsened by further declines in auto sales or future OPEC price increases.

The most telling aspect of the forecast is its confession of political bankruptcy. Commenting on the projections, Lyle Gramley of the Council of Economic Advisers told an interviewer, "Economic policy is going to stay where it is. If there were any magic levers we could pull we would have pulled them long ago."

The Administration has already pulled some levers, but to no avail. "Voluntary" wage/price guidelines merely stiffened employer resistance to wage increases while failing to slow the upward price spiral. Having seen its guidelines collapse, the Administration will now return to the orthodox inflation remedy invoked by modern capitalism: recession. But in addition to the hardship it brings to working-class Americans, that remedy presents a problem: Ever deeper recessions are needed to make even the slightest dent in inflation. The pricing policies of major corporations determine the underlying rate of inflation, and their growing market power means that declines in consumer demand are often met by price increases rather than decreases.

Despite the rhetorical laments of some Administration economists, Carter has demonstrated little real concern about our present economic state. Again, he is incapable of recognizing its dimensions. If another million Americans are laid off, there are compensating political rewards from the business community. Exxon's chairman, Clifton Garvin, says the consensus of business leaders is that "a slight recession is what we need, and this isn't all bad." Recessions historically limit the power of unions to seek wage gains.

There are other policy levers which could be pulled to control inflation and unemployment. These would involve such alternatives as increased funding of public housing (which would ease interest rates), mass transit, and community-controlled health care. Such a program would create more jobs and mitigate the structural causes of inflation. But implementation of these policies would require the Administration to place a higher priority on social needs.

Carter's crisis is described as terminal, and the search for a new savior has begun. Will it be Kennedy, Mondale, Brown,[2] or one of the Republican throwbacks to earlier, simpler times? Will it matter?

There will be one "crisis of confidence" after another for Americans and their elected Presidents as long as we cling to the notion that a band-aid here, a little patchwork there, will get us past the enormous difficulties we face. The problems intensify and the realities grow more grim. Sooner or later we will have to devise a system of politics that addresses our needs and promises to cope with the realities. Sooner would be better than later.

[2]Governor Jerry Brown of California.

Labor

22

AFL-CIO FEDERATIONIST

Coming to Grips with the Energy Crisis

August 1979

This statement appeared in the official publication of the AFL-CIO, the nation's leading labor union and a group with which Carter had uneasy relations. Keeping the interests of its members in mind, the AFL-CIO both applauded Carter's efforts and criticized those elements its leadership believed were contrary to the interests of union members and working people.

In his July 15 energy message to the nation, President Carter announced a six-point program to meet a crisis which has shaken the confidence of the American people in their government and its leaders. We agree with the thrust of the President's program. We believe that his description of the problem and the need for action spells out the urgency for sound solutions to the energy crisis. We agree with the President's call for conservation, a crash program to develop alternate sources of energy, the Energy Mobilization Board, the Energy Security Fund and for a windfall profits tax. . . .

Because of the OPEC stranglehold through price and supply decisions, the U.S. is presently at the mercy of the oil cartel, with no effective mechanism for dealing with OPEC. The giant oil companies, whose profits balloon with every OPEC price hike, have neither the incentive nor the desire to protect the American people. Only government can and must do that.

Therefore, the AFL-CIO continues to urge the creation of a government agency to:

— Determine the amount of oil to be imported;
— Negotiate its price; and

"Coming to Grips with the Energy Crisis," *AFL-CIO Federationist,* Aug. 1979, 18–19.

— Allocate it throughout the nation to best meet the needs and interests of all segments of society.

But much more must be done to solve the energy crisis, both over the short and long term.

Conservation

Conservation is of major importance in reducing the nation's dependence upon imported oil from insecure sources.

The nation must greatly expand its conservation efforts through more stringent, effective, and equitable measures. . . .

We believe that government loans, loan guarantees and grants should be available to private citizens, as well as businesses, for installation of new conservation equipment.

Alternate Energy Sources

. . . Alternate energy sources must be developed from each of the three primary categories: (1) essential renewable sources—solar, wind, gasohol, tidal and geothermal energy—for which varying degrees of technology exist and which appear to have minimal environmental effects; (2) nonrenewable sources—coal and nuclear—for which technology exists but which also pose environmental problems; and (3) new areas—such as waste matter, oil shale, tar sands, and other synthetic fuels and solar power installations—which require expensive new technology and may have potential environmental problems.

. . . No energy source should be developed without companion research into methods of reducing adverse environmental effects.

We urge that a very substantial commitment be made toward advancing solar, gasohol and other geothermal technology. . . .

The nation cannot afford to ignore coal and nuclear energy, despite environmental dangers. Greater use of scrubbers and technology to extract more energy from coal effluent, including coal regeneration, would offset air pollution through greater production of energy.

The nation must never relax stringent health and safety regulations governing nuclear power, and immediate, careful attention must be devoted to solving the problem of nuclear waste disposal. We believe that development of nuclear power must be accompanied by expanded research into technology to further reduce safety hazards so that nuclear power will enjoy the public support it must have to become a significant energy source. . . .

Energy Independence Authority

To finance the high cost of technology to develop synthetic fuels, the President has proposed a multi-billion-dollar Energy Security Fund, which we support. Since private capital has failed or refused to risk making loans to develop this technology, the federal government must provide loan guarantees, direct loans, price guarantees and be empowered to launch projects of its own, patterned after the TVA[1] concept. The federal government must also bear the responsibility and expense for expanded research into any potential environmental hazards which may result from development of synthetic fuels.

Therefore, the Energy Security Fund should be expanded into an Energy Independence Authority, with the federal government also making loan guarantees and loans for research and development of new conservation technology and production of oil and gas from public lands. . . .

Oil Prices

We believe that the President's decision to decontrol the price of oil was wrong. It will not contribute one iota to resolving the energy crisis, shorten the gas lines, or increase supplies. Control of energy prices is a legitimate responsibility of government to protect the American people from the sudden, adverse economic effects of huge energy price increases. Therefore, we support a reversal of the President's decontrol order.

With or without decontrol, there must be a windfall profits tax on the oil companies. Their gluttony has injured the American people, and inexcusable windfall profits should be put to good use through government programs to develop new sources of energy, provide added mass transit facilities and help lessen the impact of energy costs on those Americans whose incomes are insufficient to withstand higher heating oil and vehicle fuel prices. . . .

---

[1]Tennessee Valley Authority, a New Deal project that used comprehensive planning to develop a neglected region of the nation.

Other Proposals

We support the establishment of an Energy Mobilization Board to expedite construction of energy-producing facilities by eliminating red tape and unnecessary procedural delays. However, we believe this board's power must not be permitted to negate worker safety, civil rights, labor standards, anti-trust, environmental or health laws.

We call for immediate construction of the Northern Tier Pipeline to carry Alaskan oil to refineries in the Midwest. Greater shipment of domestic and foreign oil in U.S.-flag tankers, which have a proven safety record, would minimize losses due to accidents.

The loophole in the Jones Act, which allows for foreign-flag vessels to engage in commerce between the Virgin Islands and the U.S. mainland, should be closed. Oil accounts for 99 percent of the outbound shipments from the Virgin Islands to the United States. As a result of the loophole, this oil is carried in foreign-flag ships. The loophole encourages dependency on foreign ships for transportation of vital energy resources. . . .

We call for immediate legislation to prevent the giant oil companies from using federal funds to develop renewable sources of energy alternatives. We continue to support legislation to prevent oil companies from diverting their resources to acquisitions of or mergers with companies in other industries. They have abused their current monopoly powers and the nation cannot afford to be at the mercy of either the sheiks of OPEC or the barons of American oil companies. If the oil monopoly fails to adequately serve the public interest, consideration should be given to nationalization of the industry.

Environmentalists

23

THEODORE A. SNYDER JR.

Our Energy Future—A Time to Choose: Editorial

September/October 1979

Theodore Snyder, president of the Sierra Club, one of the nation's leading environmental organizations, dissented from the president's approach and argued for a more environmentally sensitive one. His response made clear that Carter's program ended the environmental movement's long honeymoon with the president.

In an effort to salvage both his political future and the nation's energy situation, President Carter has proposed a massive new program to reduce the country's dependence on foreign powers. The stakes are high: If his program is adopted by Congress after the August recess, some $140 billion may be spent over the next ten years in an attempt to reduce oil imports. But will the plan work?

President Carter may be commended for a bold attempt to confront a desperate situation, but the plan itself is far from adequate. It would result in serious damage to the environment, the economy and the nation as a whole. And it would produce too little energy that is too expensive and too late. There is, however, a positive choice that can be made—a "soft path" Alternative Energy Plan, one based on conservation and renewable sources. If adopted, it could solve our most pressing energy problems faster, cheaper and more cleanly than Carter's plan.

The President is asking Congress and the American people to support a "hard path" energy future based on nuclear power and poorly researched high-technology fossil fuels, bureaucratic decision-making and extensive environmental destruction.

The core of the President's energy plan, which is to be funded by a

Theodore A. Snyder Jr., Editorial, "Our Energy Future—A Time to Choose," *Sierra,* Sept./Oct. 1979, 4–5.

proposed tax on windfall profits from deregulation of crude oil, is a synthetic fuels production program. Some $88 billion is to be targeted for a "moon-shot" effort aimed at producing 2.5 million barrels a day (b/d) of "synfuel" by 1990—eleven years from now! (The U.S. now uses 20 million barrels of oil a day.)

Most of the synfuel would be produced by extracting liquids and gases from coal, oil shale and tar sands. The extraction processes, all highly complex and still at the infant stages of development, include retorting shale oil, and coal gasification, liquefaction and solvent extraction.

Roughly three quarters of the 2.5 million barrels a day of oil will be derived from coal and the balance from oil shale.

A crash development program, especially if accompanied by the waivers of environmental rules that Carter has proposed, would have devastating environmental consequences:

— Producing 2.5 million b/d by 1990 will require as many as 50 huge synfuel plants, each churning out 50,000 b/d. Some 37 of those plants will be fed with coal—an average of 20,000 tons a day per plant, for a total of 270 million tons a year. This would increase the current coal production rate by 33% and would magnify the already well-documented environmental impacts of coal mining.

— Oil shale production involves a staggering amount of waste rock. For every barrel of oil, about one ton of voluminous waste is produced, containing high levels of salts and toxic hydrocarbons. Reaching the President's goal of 500,000 b/d of synfuel from oil shale will involve the production and disposal of some 200 million tons of this waste a year.

— All the extraction processes are potentially extremely dirty. Solid pollutants include fly ash and furnace slag; flue gases— like those produced by coal-fired power plants—contain large amounts of sulfur oxides; "foul waters," lethal byproducts of the synfuel processes, are heavily contaminated with dissolved organic matter, phenol, ammonia, acid gases and toxic hydrocarbons.

— Synfuel production requires massive amounts of water—2 to 5 barrels of water for every barrel of synfuel derived from oil shale; 4 to 13 barrels of water per barrel of synfuel from coal. Much of the synfuel production activity will occur in the West near the coal and shale sources, where fresh water supplies—

especially underground aquifers—are extremely limited and already overdrawn.

Allocating the West's scarce water supply to synfuel production will dramatically reduce agricultural production in Colorado, Arizona, Utah, southern California and other regions. Farmland near the 50 plants will also suffer from the toxic synfuel pollutants, as will wildlife, natural vegetation, forests and even buildings.

Some of these environmental impacts can be minimized by proper safeguards: careful stripmining and reclamation; "scrubbing" sulfur oxide gas-stack emissions; and conservation and recycling to minimize excessive consumption of fresh water.

But these mitigating measures all cost money and take time to develop. They are "extras" that will probably be the first to go when Carter's crash program gets bogged down. That this fear is not just environmentalist paranoia is evidenced by Carter's proposal to create a seven-member commission—the Energy Mobilization Board—with the authority to overrule some state and local procedural requirements, as well as federal environmental regulations.

Members of Congress have also proposed mechanisms to speed approval of energy facilities. The Club recognizes the need for efficient processing of regulatory permits for new energy facilities, but the environmental, land-use and social protection gained over the last decade must not be held hostage by ill-conceived energy development proposals pushed by special interests.

The economic picture for synfuel production is equally bleak. There is a considerable delay involved; the program would produce no oil or gas for at least five years, and then only minimal production until the 1990s. Moreover, plagued with the traditional cost overruns of 300% to 400%, oil derived from synfuels will probably cost as much as $90 a barrel—that translates into $4 retail for a gallon of gasoline.

The program would provide employment for only high-technology specialists and only in some areas of the country. Finally, it would cause serious economic and sociological disruption as expanded coal production precipitates boomtown economies.

Carter's energy plan slights energy conservation and renewable energy in favor of this hard path; it simply fails to solve the nation's energy-supply problems and will result in continuing dependence on OPEC.

In contrast, the "soft path" energy plan proposed by environmentalists would alleviate both the nation's short-term and long-term supply shortages through extensive energy conservation and reliance on proven technologies for developing renewable energy sources.

Here are the highlights of the Environmental Alternative to Carter's Energy Plan:

— Increase funding for mass transit over the next ten years from the $10 billion proposed by Carter to $40 billion. This may seem like a lot of money, but it is tiny compared to the $120 billion proposed for highways during the same period.

— Invest $6.5 billion, as Carter proposes, on improving auto mileage; moreover, require greater fuel efficiency—35 mpg by 1990. This would save 750,000 barrels of oil a day.

— Spend $8 billion—not $2 billion—over the next ten years on retrofitting residential and commercial buildings with such proven energy-savers as insulation, weather stripping and efficient furnaces. This investment would save 2 million b/d at only one-third the price of each barrel of synfuel.

— Increase to $20 billion the $3.5 billion Carter has proposed for solar energy development over the next ten years. Increase Carter's $650 million for solar research to $1.2 billion for Fiscal Year 1980. Our goal should be to achieve 25% reliance on solar technologies by the year 2000.

— Through tax credits, encourage "industrial cogeneration"— industrial recycling and reuse of wasted heat and electricity. A prudent program would cost $2.5 billion a year for the next ten years—but it would conserve 1 million b/d and could eventually result in a 20% reduction in total energy use by industry.

— Invest $400 million a year for the next ten years in other methods of industrial energy conservation. The return would be a savings of one-half million b/d of oil by 1990—an energy-per-dollar yield 400% higher than from synfuels.

Other facets of this environmentally sound plan include funding a variety of other sources (such as unconventional natural-gas deposits, tertiary oil recovery research, and small hydroelectric installations), passing national legislation requiring deposits on beverage containers, and compensating low-income consumers for increased energy prices. Funding for synfuels should be cut drastically and limited to sound research.

The conservation potential of the Alternative Energy Plan is startling.

For the same level of expenditure—without significant sacrifices or changes in life-style—the conservation-oriented plan could save in the next decade four times as much imported oil as the Administration's proposal—17 billion barrels as opposed to 4.5 billion barrels. And after 1990 the Alternative Energy Plan would continue to reduce oil imports at twice the rate of the Carter proposals—9 million b/d, as opposed to 4.5 million b/d. This reduction would cut our annual oil import bill by from 45% to 55%—a saving of $35 billion to $45 billion a year. The environmental alternative would have other benefits as well. Oil prices would go down and stay down in real dollars. By 1990, the country would be well on its way to complete reliance upon renewable, environmentally sound, decentralized energy technologies.

Air quality would be significantly improved over its present level, while water quality and quantity would be preserved. Consumers would be spending much less energy to heat their houses, light their offices and drive to work.

The economy would be freed from some of the inflationary and recessionary pressures of ever-escalating energy prices, and the dollar and balance of payments situation would be improved. Local and state control over decision-making would be preserved and enhanced. And jobs, covering the full spectrum of technology levels, would be created in many fields.

The threat posed by President Carter's proposals is so great, and the need for action by every member so urgent that the board of directors has called for the mobilization of the Club's full resources for this Emergency Energy Campaign. Only a massive outpouring of grassroots concern can transform the present political climate, encouraging Congress to drop the damaging proposals and enact more rational energy alternatives. Intensive organizing efforts have already been set in motion, and letter-writing and media contacts have begun. All Sierra Club chapter and group leaders will be receiving regular updates as this campaign speeds along. You can call your local leaders (see chapter and group newsletters) for the latest details and for information on how to get involved.

Ethnic and Religious Groups

24

JEWISH WEEK

Two Cheers for a Start: Editorial

July 15, 1979

This response to Carter's speech was printed in Jewish Week, *a New York City publication that reached over 100,000 Jewish households. As this article made clear, many American Jews were acutely aware of the connection between oil supplies, energy policy, a commitment to Israel, and domestic politics.*

Having hectored and scolded Jewish leadership since the Yom Kippur War[1] for not making the energy problem the Number One item on the agenda of the American Jewish community, our applause for the belated action of 12 major Jewish organizations in urging upon President Carter a program of liberation from OPEC cannot be as wholehearted as we would like it to be.

If we offer only two of the usual quota of three cheers, it is not without unawareness of the psychological difficulties that stood in the way of reaching a Jewish consensus on the energy problem. There was, first of all, an understandable reluctance on the part of reasonable people to claim the energy crisis as a peculiarly Jewish problem. The disposition to feel that it is just another economic problem and should not require us to participate as Jews was based on plausible rationale.

Part of the Jewish hesitancy to face the energy crisis not only as Americans but as Jews was perversely due to a fear that we might be over-emphasizing our commitment to Israel, giving cynical non-Jews an excuse for concluding that all we think about is the welfare of

[1] In 1973, Egypt and Syria attacked Israel on Yom Kippur, the most sacred day of the Jewish year. Because of U.S. support for Israel, the Arab states halted oil exports to America, leading to dramatic rises in oil prices and inflation.

Editorial, "Two Cheers for a Start," *Jewish Week*, 15 July 1979, 20.

Israel, which was being threatened by the use of oil in blackmail on our foreign policy by Arab states.

Perhaps it is time, therefore, to assert that Jews feel they have a greater stake in the security, social stability and diplomatic effectiveness of the United States than any other of the nation's ethnic or religious constituent groups. While we view Israel as essential to Jewish continuity the world over and also as essential to the survival of moral civilization, we also see America, despite all its shortcomings, as the best hope for resisting successfully the powerful force threatening to turn scientific technology into instruments of dehumanizing oppression. Should America be permanently defeated by the energy challenge, there will be little hope for human freedom anywhere in the world.

As a people that has needed the freedom and the strength of this unique nation, founded upon conscience, more than any of its constituent groups, we have responded with a greater degree of civic participation both in the voting process and in the airing of public issues. It is thus our duty to strive for a consensus on the most fateful problem that has confronted our nation and, if a consensus becomes unattainable, to have at least made the effort and provided a free forum for intensive discussion.

We trust that the recommendations being offered President Carter are just the beginning of the Jewish involvement, as a community, in the search for a solution that will give America secure energy independence. The twelve organizations included in the present effort by no means complete the roster of major Jewish organizations morally obliged to deal with this issue.

Moreover, while the program outlined does surmount in some respects the cliches of "liberalism" and "conservatism" that have in the past imposed a reflexive bar to pragmatic approaches to economic problems, we would like to see a more nearly complete liberation from the attitudes of "liberalism" and "anti-liberalism" that have in the past produced closed minds.

The energy problem is really one of regaining for the American people a greater voice in determining not only the life-styles of the future, but our ability to realize the moral and cultural potential of democratic self-government. If America fails to rescue itself, the billions of deprived creatures in Asia and Africa may lose their best chance for a better life, but will there be room anywhere for Jews as Jews?

25

AMERICA

Energy Sermon: Editorial

July 28, 1979

This editorial appeared in America, *the publication of the Jesuits of the United States and Canada and a highly respected national journal among Roman Catholics. The editor both applauded Carter for emphasizing the spiritual dimensions of the nation's crisis and took issue with the policies the president proposed.*

President Carter has used the bully pulpit of the White House to call on the American people to use the energy crisis as an opportunity to "rekindle our sense of unity, our confidence in the future and [to] give our nation and all of us individually a new sense of purpose." The crisis of confidence, which he saw in the growing doubt about the meaning of our personal lives and in the loss of a unity of purpose for our nation, he characterized as a threat more serious than problems of energy or inflation. He has attempted thus to raise the problems of energy to a level higher than mere selfish squabbling over limited resources. He has placed it in the context of traditional American ideals and values, and it is in this manner that President Carter communicates with and leads the American people most effectively. This is the Mr. Carter—not the engineer and technocrat—that the American people elected.

The President traced the origin of the crisis of confidence in America to the shocks inflicted on the body politic by political assassinations, Vietnam, Watergate and the inability of the Government, whipsawed by special interests, to deal with inflation and energy. These tragedies eroded popular confidence—sometimes justifiably—in American political leaders and institutions.

The President is correct in saying that this crisis of confidence strikes at the very heart and soul and spirit of our national will. A society cannot function without trust. The social contract, whereby we are

Editorial, "Energy Sermon," *America*, 28 July 1979, 26.

bound together for the common good, breaks down when each citizen, distrusting his fellows, fights only for himself. While distrust and self-doubts were appropriate responses to Vietnam and Watergate, continued political paranoia can be just as harmful as the tragedies that caused it. Constant vigilance against abuse and misjudgments is important. But the time has come when we should be able to disagree with someone without considering him immoral and corrupt. As the President said, we simply must have faith in each other.

The President also called for a renewed faith in the future of America, the belief that the days of our children would be better than our own. This faith in progress motivated past generations to make sacrifices in hope of a better future. They believed that America was part of a great movement of humanity called democracy, involved in the search for freedom. They were proud of hard work, strong families, close-knit communities and their faith in God. All the traditions of our past and the promises of our future, said the President, point to the path of common purpose and the restoration of American values. While we cannot forget the mistakes America made in the past, President Carter rightly called upon what was great in America rather than on mere self-interest.

What was disappointing, although understandable, was the President's return in Kansas City to the metaphorical use of "war" in speaking about energy. While political scientists agree that nothing unites like a common enemy, it is naive to blame only OPEC and the oil companies for the energy shortage. In addition, while war may be a unifying image for the generation that fought World War II, it is a divisive image to the Vietnam generation. Battlefield rhetoric simply will not and should not unite people.

But the President did not just exhort. He has imposed oil import quotas so that never again will we import more oil than we did in 1977, a record high year. While quotas usually do not make much sense because they interfere with the marketplace's allocation of resources, in this case both our national security and our economic future demand reduced imports. But quotas without conservation or added domestic energy production will only cause energy shortages that will have to be allocated and rationed. The gradual decontrol of oil and gas prices will encourage both conservation and production. The windfall profits tax will encourage conservation and provide some of the money needed to fund energy conservation and production programs. An additional 50 cents to $1 a gallon tax on gasoline would also have encouraged conservation, but at a political price no one is willing to pay. Such a tax would merely have brought our gasoline prices up to the prices in the other industrialized and energy-dependent nations of the world.

There are still many unanswered questions about how the President's program will affect nuclear power plants, air pollution and other environmental issues. Everyone is against excessive red tape and against destroying the environment, but there is a long continuum between those extremes where human judgments must be made and people will disagree. Nor is it clear how much it will cost to produce synthetic oil. We can only hope that Government funds and higher energy prices will stimulate technological breakthroughs that will be both environmentally safe and not too expensive.

26

CHRISTIAN INDEX

Christians Should Lead in Conservation: Editorial

July 26, 1979

This editorial appeared in Christian Index, *the publication of the Georgia Baptist Convention, of special interest to Carter, who was himself a Georgia Baptist. It made clear how much Carter's evocation of a spiritual crisis and call for Americans to lead moral lives resonated in some sectors of the nation's Protestant community.*

President Jimmy Carter "laid it on the line" last week in calling the people of America to "a war footing" in the battle to preserve energy. Historians may record his speech as one of the turning points in political tides.

Christians of the land should lead the way in responding positively and sacrificially to President Carter's conservation appeals. His speech

Editorial, "Christians Should Lead in Conservation," *Christian Index,* 26 July 1979, 2.

played heavily on moral-spiritual-sermonic themes which should strike responsive chords in the hearts of Christians and fellow Baptists.

"A moral and spiritual crisis" is how our Southern Baptist President described the mood of America. How could any thinking citizen disagree? He also talked about crises of confidence and of will and of sacrifice. Again, who could argue with intelligence?

As Americans begin to extricate themselves from the energy quagmire, they will be called upon to make changes in lifestyles and workstyles and recreation-styles that they have never before been called to make. These changes will sorely test the moral and spiritual fiber of all of us.

Christians should take the lead in setting examples of conservation, sacrifice, unselfishness, patriotism, sharing and cooperation. And they should openly speak out in support of politicians and others who stand for conservation and sanity.

President Jimmy Carter has made us proud again that he is a Christian and a Southern Baptist. He has taken [the] reins of leadership to help lead us out of moral and spiritual crisis. He deserves our prayers and our support; also our sacrifice and our conservation.

LETTERS FROM CITIZENS

Sixty-five million Americans turned on their televisions to hear what the president had to say on July 15, 1979. Of that huge number, a small percentage (but nonetheless a significant number) sent Carter letters in response. With a speech as momentous as this, the president's advisers tracked what letter writers said and then made available to the president a carefully selected and largely favorable sample. These letters revealed not only the sense of connection some citizens felt to Carter personally and to what he said but also the often idiosyncratic lessons they took from his speech.

Correspondents frequently responded in a highly personal manner. "My wife and I," reported a husband from a suburb near Philadelphia, "thought you looked very tired. I suggest you take your family on a much needed vacation." Another writer responded sympathetically to Carter's evocation of a sense of community. Letter writers often suggested ways that Americans (including government officials) could conserve energy or expressed their own renewed determination to do so themselves. One reported trading in a gas-guzzling luxury car for a small car with a diesel engine. Many responded in more openly religious ways than the president was himself willing to acknowledge. We "plead in your behalf that God, through Jesus Christ, grant you wisdom to lead this country forward and upward," remarked a couple from Phoenix. Many urged Carter to take more determined action. Someone from Southern California called for a propaganda blitz or, if necessary, a "war-time footing." Some reacted positively to Carter as a lawgiver coming down from the mountain. "You are like a Moses trying to lead us to freedom," wrote one person from a small town in east Texas, turning Americans away from "Pagan Idols (Gas, Money + Material Things)." Many others expressed a positive view of the president's call for sacrifice, pride in America, and reassertion of the common good.*

*Letters from Citizens, Office of Staff Secretary: Presidential Handwriting File, box 139, folder "President's Address to the Nation, 7/17/79 [3] and [4]," JCPL.

27

HUGH CARTER

President's Messages of 7/15/79 and 7/16/79

July 17, 1979

Hugh Carter was the majority leader of the Georgia state senate when his cousin Jimmy Carter was governor. Serving in the White House as a special assistant for administration, Hugh provided a summary of the response from Americans as he captured the strongly positive reaction to the speech by citizens who telephoned or telegraphed the White House on July 15 and 16.

Hugh Carter to Jimmy Carter, Memorandum, "President's Messages of 7/15/79 and 7/16/79," 17 July 1979, Office of Staff Secretary: Presidential Handwriting File, box 139, folder "7/17/79, Not submitted—DF," JCPL.

MEMORANDUM FOR: THE PRESIDENT

FROM: HUGH CARTER

SUBJECT: President's Messages of 7/15/79 and 7/16/79

The cumulative total on public responses to your speeches given 7/15/79 and 7/16/79 through midnight 7/16/79 are as follows:

	#	%PRO	%CON
Telephone Calls	2,474	84	16
Telegrams (sample attached)	2,510	87	13

While general support was overwhelming, by far the most frequently mentioned subject was the public's support for your emphasis on rebuilding the American spirit.

With regard to the energy program outlined over the past two days, all action steps were supported, but the most frequently mentioned are listed below:

ISSUE	#	%PRO	%CON
Commitment to conserve.	470	85	15
Lower dependence on foreign oil by setting goals and quotas.	161	84	16
Energy Security Corporation; includes energy bonds, average Americans investing directly in America's energy security and legislation for Solar Bank.	116	83	17
Enact law so utilities cut use of oil by 50% by the end of the next decade by switching to other fuels, especially coal.	114	87	13
Authority for mandatory conservation; standby gasoline rationing; $10 billion to strengthen public transportation system and increased aid for poor/energy.	80	69	31
Congress must enact Windfall Profits Tax.	72	76	24
Energy Mobilization Board.	71	63	37
Presence of nuclear power in President's program.	47	70	30
Continued efforts toward reducing inflation by balancing the budget.	27	89	11
Mandatory compliance of oil companies with President's program.	24	83	17
Increased cooperation with Mexico and Canada.	17	82	18

Typical comments are as follows:

"Hang tough Jimmy. We'll do what we can here."—Akron, OH

"I support your proposals, do what is necessary, contact us if we can help."—Bellevue, WA

"Thank you for that strong courageous message coming straight from the heart. You put the emphasis in the right places and with you we will succeed."—Wilton, CT

"My heartfelt congratulations on your fine analysis of our national problems and sensible proposals for their solution. Have courage and our people will support you. I know it. Aloha."—Honolulu, HI

BELL, BELLAH, AND LASCH

Daniel Bell, Robert Bellah, and Christopher Lasch played formative roles in national and presidential discussions about where the nation was headed in the late 1970s. When they listened to what Carter said in his July 15 speech, each of them realized that what they had written for a wide audience and what they had said to the president personally had influenced his speech. Yet they also understood that the president had selectively adopted what each of them advocated. Their individual disappointments with what Carter said revealed much about the problems that arise when intellectuals enter the public and presidential arenas in the midst of a national crisis.

Bellah's and Lasch's reactions to the speech are included here. Bell's response also was thoughtful and complex. At the end of August 1979, he wrote to Patrick Caddell expressing his reaction. Bell objected to the notion that there was necessarily a tension between Caddell's emphasis on the moral dimensions of the crisis and Mondale's focus on the presumably more real issues of inflation and energy shortages. Bell thought that it was a mistake to say, as Carter might have been understood to have argued, that people's anxieties about rising prices and depleted savings were somehow not real. Yet Bell also countered those like Mondale who would minimize the power of underlying cultural and social trends that showed an increasing emphasis on self-regard. The task before the president, Bell argued, was to find some way to link the two approaches in a convincing manner, making clear that Carter understood the seriousness of both sets of issues. Yet in the end, although Bell hoped that the president could find a way of successfully connecting policy and fundamental cultural changes, he questioned the basic premise of such an approach and therefore of Carter's speech. It was all but impossible, he asserted, to use either a jeremiad or public policy to solve underlying cultural problems such as excessive hedonism.*

*Daniel Bell to Patrick Caddell, Letter, "Dinner at White House: Jimmy Carter/Pat Caddell, June–August 1979," 28 Aug. 1979, DBP, 3. Bell returned to these issues a few weeks later in the cover letter for his Bell, "Dinner": Daniel Bell to Pearl Bell, 1 Sept. 1979, Memoir: Dinner at the White House, Daniel Bell: Writings, September 1979, DBP.

28

ROBERT BELLAH

A Night at Camp David

July 27, 1979

Three days after the president's speech, the Berkeley sociologist gave an interview to John Raeside, a reporter with the East Bay Express *newspaper in the San Francisco Bay Area. He talked about his visit to Camp David on July 10 and about his disappointment with the speech of a president who, he believed, could not transcend or resolve the tension between his "Baptist private pietism" and "the engineer side of him."*

... When we arrived [at Camp David], ... I learned that some of ... [Carter's] top advisors had been reading some of the things I've written about the crisis of the spirit in the country—not the energy crisis. It was conveyed to us that one of the reasons for Carter's decision to cancel the speech that had been scheduled for July 5th was that he didn't want just to talk about the technicalities of energy; he wanted to put it in a larger context. ...

Well, we then went into a large conference room, and the President opened with a prayer. Actually, it was kind of embarrassing because he talked about how we "all shared Christian Fellowship" and there was Marc Tanenbaum of the American Jewish Committee so it wasn't ecumenical enough. But either he caught it or Rosalynn caught it because he asked Marc to give the closing prayer.

Robert Bellah, "A Night at Camp David," *East Bay Express,* 27 July 1979, 1, 3, and 4.

After the prayer, Carter gave a little opening statement saying that the larger issues were very much on his mind, and that he didn't want to give the speech without reflecting about them. And he talked about how he was feeling a little lonely. He said he was not in a state of despair, he was not feeling a lack of self-confidence, but he *was* feeling a little lonely—which I think you have to say is a fair statement. In response to that, most of the people who spoke—well, everyone spoke—but most of us opened with something like, "I know it's tough to be where you are right now," or, "The problem is not just yours, etcetera, etcetera, we're all in this together. . . ."

. . . On the whole, the President listened; he didn't say very much. He did interrupt on two or three occasions. One time I remember that particularly struck me was when I said I was glad that "you didn't just give a speech that said OPEC was at fault and that we're going to solve it with a big technological push," and he said, "It would be rather self-righteous to blame it all on OPEC." He said, "Americans don't like it when a foreign country can interfere in our life, but we've been interfering in OPEC countries' and most other countries' lives rather heavily for a long time."

. . . I can't imagine Nixon or Ford even admitting that privately. They'd say, "We don't interfere in other countries, we only help them." No, Carter does know some things about the real world.

I was one of the last people to speak and he asked me specifically, "Bob, what should I say? How much can the American people take?"

Well, that really seemed to be what was on their minds. They wanted to say something about the deeper problems, but they were also concerned with the strategic issue: Will it backfire? How much will go? I made a fairly impassioned statement asking for almost a Jeremiah. I said I felt people wanted to be told that it was all OPEC's fault and that some kind of technology would solve everything—but that they knew it was a lie. We'd like to believe it, but on a deeper level we know it isn't true. I said that I thought genuine and true leadership would say what is true and not just what people want to hear. I urged him to be what I've called in my work "a teaching President," one who points out what it means to maintain our tradition in a given historic period . . . who gives us something new as well as something that continues what is old. Tell us the hard truths—don't just tell people what they want to hear. That's not what a teaching president is.

Marc Tanenbaum was one of my big allies, in fact he attacked the free enterprise system, and Claire Randall[1] was quite critical of our

---

[1] Executive secretary of the National Council of Churches.

basic institutions. We all said, "Look, don't just invoke spiritual values and sacrifice if you're not going to say something about the structural conditions that force people to be more selfish than they might want to be, like building the whole economy on the profit motive." We didn't really expect him to say *that*, but *something* like that.

In closing, he said that the whole meeting and particularly the last half hour—that's when both Marc Tanenbaum and I had spoken in the strongest terms about our critical evaluation of what was happening in the country—had been the most informing thing in the whole sequence. Then he called on Marc to give the closing prayer and he said "Let's all hold hands." So we were all holding hands, and Marc gave a lovely prayer—it was the type of prayer that *is* a prayer, but it also gets the message across one last time, if you know what I mean? . . .

So it was kind of an up experience, and I came away feeling . . . well, I had felt during the campaign that maybe . . . you see, the biggest problem with Carter is that he's an honest man, a man with some integrity, perhaps the most decent human being who's been in that office for quite awhile. But he doesn't know how to translate that into politics. He has no social vision. There's a kind of personal integrity, there's a Baptist private pietism. But when it comes to politics, he's too quick to rely on technocrats. Some kind of gimmick, some kind of reorganization of government . . . it's the engineer side of him, the side of him that went to Annapolis. It's a strategy rather than politics. There's no translation of morality into a kind of politics that would be mobilizational in more than a superficial sense, because that would involve genuine input and participation from people. But I'd hope that, you know, maybe after two-and-a-half years in office, and watching the polls go down, that maybe he would have learned through experience that relying on the technocrats had gotten him into a terrible mess, and that maybe he would turn his conscience into something more socially viable.

Well, I would say [when I left Camp David] that I wasn't immensely optimistic. I could see all the limitations. But I was, nonetheless, very moved by this experience. . . .

But it was with some fear and trembling that I sat down to listen to Carter's speech on Sunday night, and I was just really down on it. It just didn't make it. He threw in a phrase or two like "moral and spiritual crisis," and attached too much emphasis on self-interest and narrow lobbies, but Carter didn't put together any picture that to me had any real coherence. On the moral malaise issue, he starts off by going back to his campaign rhetoric, about how wonderful the American people are, about how the U.S. needs "a government as good as its people," and he says that "the trouble is we're isolated in Washington, we've got to go back to the people, get in touch with what wonderful and moral people they really are" . . . then suddenly we hear all this about how we don't have any confidence, we don't have any faith, we don't believe in the future, we're not saving, productivity's down . . . well, what's happening here? How come all these wonderful people have all these bad characteristics? No analysis! No putting things together. Flattery and criticism.

I didn't want to hear about how wonderful the American people are, because I think the American people have precisely the government they deserve. It's time to lay it on the line and deal with something more than this phony criticism of Washington. So I was just deeply and basically disappointed.

And then on the technical issues, I don't know. I'm not a specialist, but Carter seemed to have no sense of the array of options and of the social, moral and spiritual cost of choosing one option over another. "We're going to have everything; we're going to have the shale, we're going to have coal, we're going to have solar . . . we'll have it all." But what is it going to cost? Economically? Politically? What are the social consequences? Everything but the kitchen sink is thrown in. We're going to have a crash program. And what does he want us to do? "Say something nice about the country every day." . . .

He could have said: Look, we've had a great history, we've satisfied a lot of needs, we've done a lot of terrible things too but, by and large, we've been one of the most decent societies in human history . . . and we've done it all by combining an ethic of deep concern for other human beings with an ethic of everybody looking out for Number One. And it's worked. *But it's not going to work anymore.* We're up against a new world, a new kind of situation, a new set of limits—ecological, political, economic—and we're not going to be able to afford the totally unlimited self-indulgence and kind of economic system that feeds that self-indulgence any longer. Our choices are two: either we're going to solve it by authoritarianism, with a government that tells us what we can consume and what we're not going to be allowed to do, or we're going to solve it through a reorganization of our society along volunteeristic lines in accordance with our long tradition of democratic process. It's not going to be easy, because most of the basic interests of our society will have to be reoriented. Now I don't have any answers. I can't tell you what to do today. We're going to be working on this for the rest of the century *at least*. But what I'm saying is *it's not going to be like it was!* And we'd better start thinking about what it's going to be. The best thing is to involve the whole nation in some kind of serious consideration of what the options are as we move into a different world.

Well, that's not what he said. He said, "You can have everything. You can have it all. Oh, you may have to turn off the lights a bit, but basically there's nothing to be scared of. We've had harder problems many times before." But we've never had harder problems! We've never had a crisis that requires a fundamental reorientation of our values like this. He just did not take the tough line.

. . . By trying to compromise everything, and not take a tough position on anything, I think it's all just cosmetic and it's not going to change the fundamental loss of confidence that the people have in him. . . .

. . . The whole war analogy is basically false. The moral equivalent of war is a great idea, but to push it as hard as he did . . . what he was really trying to evoke was World War II. Much of the imagery was straight out of World War II. Well, I think that's very misleading as an analogy. World War II was probably the one time in our entire history when the moral issue was absolutely clear. We were faced with the worst social system that has ever been created by human beings, and it was outside; our basic problem was how to mobilize ourselves to oppose this external danger. This crisis is not outside. OPEC did not create it. We gave OPEC its power over us through our own decisions. This is a crisis . . . a profound crisis of the internal structures of American values in society. So the war image doesn't work. It's an evasion, and to use the war image and then to assume that the real answer to the problem is morale boosting—you know, "Let's have faith again" and "Let's have confidence again"—to me that's pathetic.

The last moment when genuine moral leadership was generated and was effective, at least partially effective, on the American scene was the Civil Rights Movement. And there the great leader was not a President, it was Martin Luther King. It was King who led a movement that involved millions of people and that finally led to the passage of the legislation that John Kennedy had never been able to push through. That legislation changed some fundamental things. I mean there's a lot that's still wrong, but if you are old enough to remember what it was like for blacks in this country before 1950, you know that there's been a dramatic change. Now that was a change that resulted from a mobilization of people, a change of consciousness that finally culminated in something that changed our basic institutions.

But it seems to me that [the] kind of situation we're now in is much more complicated than the Civil Rights Movement. It requires changing consciousness. It's not just a question of making the right technological decisions—it involves mobilizing people, it involves facing difficult issues that are going to arouse lots of hostility and hatred. The notion that we're going to get through all of this through just harmony and morale is nuts. Too many interests are going to have to be pinched if we're going to do it democratically. Now I don't know whether any President could lead that kind of movement. Probably if it's going to be successful, it will have to achieve a balance between movements that are not directly tied to presidential politics and some kind of political leadership that can respond to it. . . .

. . . Carter came to the verge of telling us that [there's nobody in the White House who's going to solve all of our problems]. What he should have said is, "Don't look to the White House, the whole damn country is problematic. We've got to rethink a lot of things." Sure, there should be some direction and help from the leadership, but only through some kind of public process that involves everyone can we ever get through this. . . .

29

CHRISTOPHER LASCH

Letter to Patrick Caddell

July 18, 1979

The author of The Culture of Narcissism *(1979) wrote three letters to the White House—one to Jody Powell in June 1979 and two after the July 15 speech to Patrick Caddell. In the first letter to Caddell, which follows, Lasch applauded the way the president connected "moral and cultural issues" with economic ones even as he pressed Carter to adopt a more radical and populist approach.*

Christopher Lasch to Patrick Caddell, Letter, 18 July 1979, box 20, folder 6, Christopher Lasch Papers, Department of Rare Books and Special Collections, University of Rochester Library, University of Rochester, Rochester, N.Y.

Dear Pat:

A number of reporters have asked me to comment on the President's speech, but I have turned down a request for an interview with CBS News and refrained from all but the most guarded comments elsewhere, fearing that any reservations I might express could all too easily be misinterpreted and misused. The tenor of the questions put to me suggests that, as usual, the media are less interested in a frank discussion of the issues raised by the speech than in the inside story of how it came to be written, in sampling "reactions" to the President's "performance," and in gearing up for the next presidential campaign. Under these circumstances I think they might for their own reasons welcome criticism of the President, or even anything that could be construed as criticism, from a left-wing author claiming that his ideas had been misused, bowdlerized,[1] or put to purposes he had not intended and could not now countenance. Though it would be easy to indulge their insatiable appetite for "critical commentary"—and in my own case to forestall charges from the Left that I've been seduced and coopted by too close proximity to power—it is increasingly clear that the real danger of cooptation, these days, comes from the media, which absorb and homogenize all points of view and turn them to the purpose of political entertainment. So I address these remarks to you instead of putting them out for general consumption—the word could not be more appropriate in this context.

The speech itself seemed to me courageous, powerful, and often moving—better in some ways than the policies it announced. It struck a note of moral earnestness that has made a strong impact on everyone I've talked to (barring reporters), even among people who haven't counted themselves among the President's supporters. It managed to speak realistically about the country's troubles without invoking a mood of panic or national emergency. Instead of pleading for broad executive power, it insisted on the limits of federal action—even while accepting responsibility for bold and expensive measures. Best of all, it sought to connect moral and cultural issues on the one hand with economic issues on the other. Such is the stupidity that prevails among the political commentators and pundits, that what was clearly intended as an analysis of the link between the "crisis of confidence" and the energy crisis has been widely misunderstood—and in some quarters dismissed—as a "sermon." Perhaps it is only the sophisti-

---

[1] Removing from a document material that is considered improper.

cated and overeducated (that is, half-educated and semiliterate) members of society who confuse sermons with empty moralizing and platitudinous exhortation, and who don't see (having lost touch with this country's Calvinist heritage) that a sermon can have great analytical depth and political force. It is only to the metropolitan mind—more provincial than the provincialisms it scorns—that a "sermon" presents itself as a term of dismissal and contempt.

That brings me to the main point of this letter: the need to confront more openly, though not in any spirit of demagoguery or anti-intellectualism, the social divisions in this country, and to address more directly the groups that have a real stake in change—poor people, working-class people, and any others whose minds have not been wholly paralyzed by the culture of "self-expression" and self-gratification. I don't think there is much to be gained from appeals for national unity. Nor do I see much point in denouncing the selfishness of special interests. It's true that Congress is too responsive to special interest groups, but the reasons for this have more to do with underlying changes in the political system than with the undeniable rapacity and greed of special interests. A more serious problem, it seems to me, is the ascendancy of corporate interests *as a whole,* and more broadly of the managerial and professional elite that gets most of the social and economic advantages from the existing distribution of power. What I have called the culture of narcissism is above all the culture of this class. These people have sold the rest of us on their way of life, but it is their way of life first and foremost, and it reflects their values, their rootless existence, their craving for novelty and contempt for the past, their confusion of reality with electronically mediated images of reality, their essentially gossipy approach to politics, their "other-directed"[2] round of life and the bureaucratic setting (corporate or governmental) in which it unfolds.

Appeals for hard work, discipline, and sacrifice are likely to fall on deaf ears when addressed, not to those who most need to hear them, but to people who already work hard and undergo sacrifices every day through no choice of their own. Such appeals will only reinforce the prevailing cynicism unless coupled with an attack—more than a rhetorical attack—on the power and privileges of elites. A few years ago, many Americans patriotically turned down their thermostats in the winter only to be socked with higher fuel prices, justified on the

---

[2]In *The Lonely Crowd* (1950), David Riesman used the phrase "other-directed" to refer to people who were acutely sensitive to the opinions of others.

grounds that demand was off. This is not the kind of experience that restores people's faith in industry or government. I think it has to be made clear, in short, that sacrifices are going to be apportioned according to the capacity to bear them, in accordance with elementary principles of justice.

Beyond that, a serious discussion has to take place—has to begin—about the kind of energy policy, and the kind of economic institutions—that would best serve the needs of rudimentary fairness. What kind of energy policies would be most likely to preserve the gross inequalities in the present distribution of wealth and power? What kind of policies would contribute, on the other hand, to a more democratic distribution of wealth and power? I'm not advocating a centrally imposed equality of condition, but its opposite: the kind of decentralization that would break up existing concentrations of power and approximate the general diffusion of property regarded by the Founding Fathers as the indispensable underpinning of republican institutions.

In his Sunday night speech, the President rightly said that we stand at a turning point in our history. But I think the choices confronting us could be formulated more pointedly. He spoke of a choice between self-aggrandizement (a "mistaken idea of freedom") and the "restoration of American values." I would be more specific. The choice is between centralization and concentration of power on the one hand, localism and "participatory democracy" on the other—and participatory democracy remains a good idea, no matter how outrageously the New Left[3] may have perverted it. I suspect that policies which don't demonstrably contribute to the second kind of solution will not arouse much enthusiasm over the long run—except among groups that stand to gain from more centralization, more consumerism, more self-defeating technology.

I can't claim to speak with authority about the energy problem as such, but it doesn't take much wit to see that the only feasible policy in the long run is one based on renewable resources and minimal damage to the environment. This kind of policy commends itself for two reasons: because it best serves the interests of localism and democracy, and because it best serves the interests of future generations, who will have to live with the consequences of decisions made today even though they had no hand in making them. A centralized policy

[3]Student radicals in the 1960s, most notably members of Students for a Democratic Society (SDS).

relying heavily on nuclear power and other synthetic fuels is objectionable not only because it perpetuates the morally indefensible concentration of power and wealth (benefitting the very companies that have already brought us to the current critical pass) but because it mortgages the future to the immediate interests of the present generation.

This is the ultimate indictment of the "culture of narcissism"—not that it is self-indulgent and self-absorbed but because it is criminally indifferent to the welfare of the next generation and the generation after that. In my book, I tried to show that this irresponsibility turns up in many forms (especially among the professional and managerial elite): in the criminally negligent way we educate our children, in the refusal of parents to discipline or make any moral demands on the young, in the way we exalt immediate sexual pleasure over reproduction, etc. But this disregard of the future also shows itself, most clearly of all, in the way we squander precious resources without any regard for those who will inherit our over-fond self-regard. Looked at from this point of view, the notion of "renewable resources"—whatever the merely faddish environmentalism with which it is sometimes associated—has a lot to tell us about the choice confronting us and the new direction our society ought to take.

Yours,

Kit

Christopher Lasch

POLITICAL OPPOSITION

Even though Ted Kennedy and Ronald Reagan came from opposite ends of the political spectrum, these two challengers to the president played on Carter's weaknesses, which many found so clear in the "crisis of confidence" speech.

Elected to the U.S. Senate in 1962 at age thirty and heir to the presidential ambitions of two older brothers who were assassinated, Senator Edward M. Kennedy had considered running for the presidency in 1968, 1972, and 1976. In November 1979, he announced that he would oppose Carter in the 1980 Democratic primaries. Kennedy thus took on the role of the spoiler who might prevent and would certainly complicate the reelection of a sitting president of his own party. He contested the renomination of Carter for a number of reasons, including the president's problematic leadership and his own commitment to more progressive positions on labor, consumer protection, health care, and civil rights. In the ensuing months, Kennedy's campaign stumbled, as he himself performed poorly on TV and in early contests. At the same time, the president gained support following the Soviet invasion of Afghanistan and the seizure of U.S. hostages in Iran.

To the president's right, two Republicans challenged Carter for the presidency in 1979 and 1980. Eventually, former governor of Texas John Connally faded, and Ronald Reagan won his party's nomination. Once a movie actor, Reagan had served as governor of California from 1967 to 1975. On foreign policy, as the speech he delivered on November 3, 1980, made clear, the forcefully anti-Communist Reagan opposed Carter's desire to reach accommodation with the Soviet Union. On domestic issues, Reagan opposed Carter's attempt to use federal policy to engineer the economy, most notably on energy issues. Instead, he believed that getting the government off the backs of citizens would unleash private enterprise, which in turn would solve economic and social problems more effectively than intervention from Washington.

30

EDWARD M. KENNEDY

Speech

November 7, 1979

Three days after American hostages were taken in Iran, at historic Faneuil Hall in Boston, Kennedy announced that he would challenge Carter for the presidential nomination of the Democratic party. He offered himself, in obvious contrast to Carter, as a forceful national leader who would protect American interests abroad. He made clear that he would avoid blaming Americans for being selfishly "mired in malaise" and instead would pay particular attention to the plight of the nation's most disadvantaged citizens.

Today I speak to all the citizens of America. But I wanted to speak to you from home, here in Boston. In this hall, where John Hancock and

Edward M. Kennedy, Speech, *Boston Globe,* 8 Nov. 1979, 8.

Sam Adams first stirred the American Revolution, I see the faces of some who accompanied my grandfather[1] as he campaigned for Congress—long before I was born—along the crowded, North End streets visible from these windows. When I was six years old he would walk with me through this neighborhood he loved—down Ferry to North street and then to Garden Court, where my mother Rose was born.

Here, also, are the faces of childhood memory, and of many friends and loyal supporters who have been by my side through almost two decades of public life.

It was here, to this city, that my ancestors came, looking for new opportunities in a new world.

So powerful was the attraction of this land that thousands, and then millions, abandoned all that was familiar. They made the perilous journey across the sea, seeking a brighter destiny in a distant continent.

Every generation has struggled to preserve the old dream against new dangers. And now it is our turn.

I was taught long ago that politics is a noble occupation, that public service is among the most honorable of professions.

This conviction has been reinforced by almost two decades in the United States Senate. As a senator, I've taken positions on thousands of issues. I gladly offer that record as witness to my qualifications for higher office.

But the Senate has provided more than an education in the challenges of our time. It has also been my school in the way good intentions can be translated to achievement. There I have learned the necessary ways of persuasion and conciliation.

I have learned to deal with the continental diversity of interests that my colleagues have been elected to represent—fishermen in Massachusetts and farmers in Iowa, construction workers in California and small businessmen and women in Pennsylvania, oil workers in Texas and timber workers in Alabama.

There is a chance for high achievement in the Congress. I am grateful for the many occasions the Senate has given me for service to Massachusetts and to the country.

But when present difficulties grow so large that they threaten the essential confidence of the nation, the energies of our people must be marshalled toward a larger purpose—and that can only be done from the White House. Only the President can provide the sense of direction

---

[1] Kennedy's maternal grandfather, John "Honey Fitz" Fitzgerald was a legendary Boston politician who served in the U.S. House of Representatives and as the city's mayor.

needed by the nation. Only the President can inspire the common will to reach our goals.

For many months, we have been sinking into crisis. Yet, we hear no clear summons from the center of power. Aims are not set. The means of realizing them are neglected. Conflicts in directions confuse our purpose. Government falters. Fear spreads that our leaders have resigned themselves to retreat.

This country is not prepared to sound retreat. It is ready to advance. It is willing to make a stand. And so am I.

And therefore, I take the course compelled by events and by my commitment to public life. Today, I formally announce that I am a candidate for President of the United States.

I question no man's intentions. But I have a different view of the highest office in the land—a view of a forceful, effective presidency, in the thick of the action, at the center of all the great concerns our people share.

The failures are stark:

— Workers are forced to take a second job to make ends meet, because wages are rising only half as fast as prices.
— Families go into debt and suffer real financial hardship to educate their children.
— This year, the poorest 10 percent of our population must pay 119 percent of their income for the necessities of life. That means they go without.

And such distress reaches far beyond the plight of the poor. It clouds the future for millions in our society who have worked, and worked hard, to make their way, and who now see that America has begun to let them down.

The numbers and projections help us to know what is happening. But they do not tell the stories of hardship and deprivation, of defeated expectations and discarded dreams: the elderly walled in, living out their years on pensions worth less and less; the young couple who can no longer afford the home for which they have saved since marriage; the policeman and his wife who lavished so much hope and love for the future of a child who cannot now go to college.

We are only beginning to understand these causes of distress. The solutions we seek may follow unfamiliar paths. But there is one direction in which this path does not lead. It does not mean any departure from the principles of the Democratic Party, or the convictions so rooted in the life of my family and in my own career.

I am fully committed to the principle of equal opportunity. Government must take active responsibility to guarantee that opportunity is neither diminished nor denied for any Americans because they are women, or because they are black or because they were born to the Spanish tongue.

I am fully committed to the principle of progress for the poor and helpless. We can say, and truly so, that we cannot solve any of our problems by throwing money at them. But we must develop more effective answers in areas such as education and jobs, especially for the young now entering the world of work, and measures to make our cities places where people can live in dignity and safety.

I am fully committed to a program to end the spiraling costs of health care—and to guarantee that the desperation of serious illness shall not be aggravated by the fear of financial ruin. We must free every citizen from that fear.

And I am fully committed to a more coherent foreign policy, one that will speak again with a clear and consistent voice to every other nation. Our friends must trust the steady course of our purpose. Our adversaries must know that our defense will always be sufficient beyond doubt to protect our own land and our allies.

Above all else, I am fully committed to a fair and prosperous economy at home, and to a forceful pursuit of our economic interests overseas.

Surely, the nation that came back from the Depression a half a century ago can roll back the tides of inflation. Surely a nation with our talents and gifts can launch a new era of competition and innovation, equal to any in our past. Surely we are not helpless to protect the dollar and prevent other nations from holding our economy hostage to their products. Let us make clear that we stand always ready to be a partner, but that we shall never be a victim.

Everyone agrees that we need an energy policy. But not just any policy. We need a policy which [has] not yet been put in place. One imaginative enough to bring our citizens to conserve old sources of energy, while we speed the pursuit of new forms of energy, including power from the sun. We need not be permanent beggars at the banquet tables of the OPEC rulers. Nor should we rush to embrace a nuclear future until we are certain this will not threaten the future itself.

Before the last election, we were told that Americans were honest, loving, good, decent, and compassionate. Now, the people are blamed for every national ill, scolded as greedy, wasteful, and mired in malaise.

Which is it? Did we change so much in these three years? Or is it because our present leadership does not understand that we are willing, even anxious, to be on the march again.

I seek the presidency with no illusions. The most important task of presidential leadership is to release the native energy of the people. The only thing that paralyzes us today is the myth that we cannot move. If Americans are pessimistic, it is because they are also realistic. They have made a fair judgment on how government is doing — and they are demanding something better.

Where there is vision, the people respond. We must restore the faith of citizens that the system can be made to work if they will make government work for them.

I approach this task with confidence in our capacity to open widening horizons of opportunity and destiny. I set out today, heartened by the lesson of history that failure is not an American habit. I hold many public beliefs, but one above all else: I believe in the hope and the daring that have made this country great.

Thomas Wolfe[2] once wrote:

> So then to all persons their chance
> to work to be themselves,
> and to become
> whatever thing their humanity and their vision
> can combine to make them.
> This, seeker, is the promise of America.

Let us carry forward the golden promise that is America. And if we succeed at that, then someday we can look back and say that this hall was rightly chosen for this day by renewing the promise of our forebears. We will have earned our place on this platform.

---

[2]Thomas Wolfe (1900–1938) was an American novelist. The quote is from his book *You Can't Go Home Again* (1940).

31

RONALD REAGAN

A Vision for America

November 3, 1980

On November 3, 1980, the day before he defeated Carter in the 1980 presidential election, Ronald Reagan spelled out his vision for America. Like Ted Kennedy, Reagan countered Carter's vision of an America trapped in a malaise or spiritual crisis. Instead, he evoked a new day for the nation, in which strength abroad and limits on the federal government's power at home would restore America's greatness, confidence, and prosperity.

... A child born this year will begin his or her adult life in what will be the 21st century. What kind of country, what kind of legacy will we leave to these young men and women who will live out America's third century as a nation? ...

Many of us are unhappy about our worsening economic problems, about the constant crisis atmosphere in our foreign policy, about our diminishing prestige around the globe, about the weakness in our economy and national security that jeopardizes world peace, about our lack of strong, straight-forward leadership.

And many Americans today, just as they did 200 years ago, feel burdened, stifled and sometimes even oppressed by government that has grown too large, too bureaucratic, too wasteful, too unresponsive, too uncaring about people and their problems.

Americans, who have always known that excessive bureaucracy is the enemy of excellence and compassion, want a change in public life—a change that makes government work *for* people. They seek a vision of a better America, a vision of a society that frees the energies and ingenuity of our people while it extends compassion to the lonely, the desperate, and the forgotten.

I believe we can embark on a new age of reform in this country and

Ronald Reagan, Speech, "A Vision for America," 3 Nov. 1980, Ronald Reagan Library, Simi Valley, Calif.

an era of national renewal. An era that will reorder the relationship between citizen and government, that will make government again responsive to people, that will revitalize the values of family, work, and neighborhood and that will restore our private and independent social institutions. These institutions always have served as both buffer and bridge between the individual and the state—and these institutions, not government, are the real sources of our economic and social progress as a people.

That's why I've said throughout this campaign that we must control and limit the growth of federal spending, that we must reduce tax rates to stimulate work and savings and investment. That's why I've said we can relieve labor and business of burdensome, unnecessary regulations and still maintain high standards of environmental and occupational safety. That's why I've said we can reduce the cost of government by eliminating billions lost to waste and fraud in the federal bureaucracy—a problem that is now an unrelenting national scandal. And because we are a Federation of sovereign states, we can restore the health and vitality of state and local governments by returning to them control over programs best run at those levels of government closer to the people. We can fight corruption while we work to bring into our government women and men of competence and high integrity. . . .

. . . I am confident we can . . . get government off our backs, out of our pockets and up to the standards of decency and excellence envisioned by the founding fathers.

But beyond even these reforms—as important as they are—there is something more, much more, that needs to be said tonight.

That's why I want to talk with you—not about campaign issues—but about America, about us, you and me.

Not so long ago, we emerged from a world war. Turning homeward at last, we built a grand prosperity and hoped—from our own success and plenty—to help others less fortunate.

Our peace was a tense and bitter one, but in those days the center seemed to hold.

Then came the hard years: riots and assassinations, domestic strife over the Vietnam War and in the last four years, drift and disaster in Washington.

It all seems a long way from a time when politics was a national passion and sometimes even fun. . . .

That is really the question before us tonight: for the first time in our memory many Americans are asking: does history still have a place for America, for her people, for her great ideals? There are some who answer "no"; that our energy is spent, our days of greatness at an end, that a great national malaise is upon us.

They say we must cut our expectations, conserve and withdraw, that we must tell our children . . . not to dream as we once dreamed. . . .

Do not mistake me, no reasonable man who sees the world as it is, who views the deterioration of our economy, the waning of our relationships with our allies, the growth of Soviet might and the sufferings of our recent past could underestimate the difficulties before us.

But I wonder if those who doubt America have forgotten that just as in the lives of individuals so too in the lives of nations: it is always when things seem most unbearable—that we must have faith that America's trials have meaning beyond our own understanding.

Since her beginning America has held fast to this hope of divine providence, this vision of "man *with* God."

It is true that world peace is jeopardized by those who view man— not as a noble being—but as an accident of nature, without soul, and important only to the extent he can serve an all powerful state.

But it is our spiritual commitment—more than all the military might in the world—that will win our struggle for peace.

It is not "bombs and rockets" but belief and resolve—it is humility before God that is ultimately the source of America's strength as a nation. . . .

During this last year, I have had a chance to meet and talk on the campaign trail with Americans in every corner of the United States.

I find no national malaise, I find nothing wrong with the American people. Oh, they are frustrated, even angry at what has been done to this blessed land. But more than anything they are sturdy and robust as they have always been.

Any nation that sees softness in our prosperity or disunity—in our sometimes noisy arguments with each other—let such nations not make the mistakes others have made—let them understand that we will put aside in a moment the fruits of our prosperity and the luxury of our disagreements if the cause is a safe and peaceful future for our children.

Let it always be clear that we have no dreams of empire, that we seek no manifest destiny, that we understand the limitations of any one nation's power.

But let it also be clear that we do not shirk history's call; that America is not turned inward but outward—toward others. Let it be clear that we have not lessened our commitment to peace or to the hope that someday all of the people of the world will enjoy lives of decency, lives with a degree of freedom, with a measure of dignity.

Together, tonight, let us say what so many long to hear: that America is still united, still strong, still compassionate, still clinging fast to the dream of peace and freedom, still willing to stand by those who are persecuted or alone. . . .

Tomorrow morning, you will be making a choice between different visions of the future. Your decision is a uniquely personal one. It belongs to no one but you. It will be critical in determining the path we will follow in the years ahead.

If you feel that Mr. Carter has faithfully served America with the kind of competence and distinction which deserve four more years in office, then you should vote for him. If he has given you the kind of leadership you are looking for, if he instills in you pride for our country and a sense of optimism about our future, then he should be reelected.

But consider these questions as well when you finally make your decision:

Are you more confident that our economy will create productive work for our society or are you less confident? Do you feel you can keep the job you have or gain a job if you don't have one?

Are you satisfied that inflation at the highest rates in 33 years were [sic] the best that we could do? Are interest rates at 14½ percent something you are prepared to live with?

Are you pleased with the ability of young people to buy a home; of the elderly to live their remaining years in happiness; of our youngsters to take pride in the world we have built for them?

Is our nation stronger and more capable of leading the world toward peace and freedom or is it weaker?

Is there more stability in the world or less?

Are you convinced that we have earned the respect of the world and our allies, or has America's position across the globe diminished?

Are you personally more secure in your life? Is your family more secure? Is America safer in the world?

And, most importantly—quite simply—the basic question of our lives: are you happier today than when Mr. Carter became President of the United States?

I cannot answer those questions for you. Only you can.

It is autumn now in Washington, and the residents there say that more than ever during the past few years, Americans are coming to visit their capital—some say because economic conditions rule out more expensive vacations elsewhere; some say an election year has heightened interest in the workings of the national government.

Others say something different: in a time when our values, when our place in history is so seriously questioned, they say Americans want their sons and daughters to see what is still for them and for so many other millions in the world a city offering the "last best hope of man on earth"!

You can see them—these Washington visitors—looking for the famous as they walk through congressional hallways; see them as they return silent and tightlipped to tour buses that brought them for a walk through rows of white crosses in Arlington Cemetery; you can see them as they look up at a towering statue of Jefferson or out from the top of the Washington Monument; or as they read the words inscribed at the Lincoln Memorial. "Let us bind up the nation's wounds."

These visitors to that city on the Potomac do not come as white or black, red or yellow; they are not Jews or Christians; conservatives or liberals; or Democrats or Republicans. They are Americans awed by what has gone before, proud of what for them is still . . . a shining city on a hill.

At this very moment, some young American, coming up along the Virginia or Maryland shores of the Potomac, is seeing for the first time the lights that glow on the great halls of our government and the monuments to the memory of our great men.

Let us resolve tonight that young Americans will always see those Potomac lights; that they will always find there a city of hope in a country that is free. And let us resolve they will say of our day and of our generation that we did keep faith with our God, that we did act "worthy of ourselves"; that we did protect and pass on lovingly that shining city on a hill.

6
Looking Back

For the rest of the twentieth century and into the twenty-first, Carter's "crisis of confidence" speech—and the issues surrounding it—became a lodestar for politicians and political commentators. In 1980, *New York Times* columnist Francis X. Clines remarked that soon after the speech, Carter "was nailed by critics to a cross of malaise."* Under the title "How to Lose the Next Election: Americans Won't Choose a President Who Chides Them," Kevin Baker wrote in a 2000 issue of *American Heritage* that as "the most widely remembered presidential scold," Carter "was soon sent packing."†

Jimmy and Rosalynn Carter felt differently. The first lady remembered the speech as "profound and effective." She was "delighted," she noted in her memoir, "when the public opinion polls indicated that people had responded to Jimmy's words just as we had hoped."‡ In a 1982 interview, Jimmy Carter noted that the press "erroneously" called his July 15 talk "the 'malaise' speech." It was, he insisted, "the most successful speech I ever made. It had the largest viewing audience and the highest approbation of any speech I've ever made in my life."§

Early in the presidency of George W. Bush, an energy crisis that never fully materialized loomed on the horizon throughout the summer of 2001 as rolling blackouts in California forced millions to cope without electricity for hours at a time. Once again, many of the same energy issues that arose in 1979 commanded attention. As they had in the 1970s, politicians and political observers argued over whether con-

---

*Francis X. Clines, "Candidates Also Appeal to Those Basic Virtues," *New York Times,* 26 Oct. 1980, sec. E, p. 2.

†Kevin Baker, "How to Lose the Next Election: Americans Won't Choose a President Who Chides Them," *American Heritage,* Feb./Mar. 2000, 14.

‡Rosalynn Carter, *First Lady from Plains* (Boston: Houghton Mifflin, 1984), 303.

§Jimmy Carter, Interview, 29 Nov. 1982, Miller Center Interviews, box 1, Miller Center of Public Affairs, JCPL, 65.

servation was a personal virtue or an important component of national energy policy. They debated the relative merits of coal, nuclear power, imported oil, and increased domestic production. Some wondered, as Carter and others had in 1979, whether Americans' affluence had lulled them into a complacency that made sacrifice and simple living unthinkable. Others questioned the nation's resolve to conquer its energy problems with the same mobilization of resources that had produced the atomic bomb in the 1940s. Finally, some people returned to the wider issues of 1979—the Arab-Israeli dispute, Islamic fundamentalism, and Middle East oil—with post-9/11 terrorism eventually added to this already potent mix.

32

DICK CHENEY

Speech

April 30, 2001

Vice President Dick Cheney, like President George W. Bush, came to the White House with experience in the oil and natural gas industries. Early in the Bush administration, Cheney recalled Carter's attack on American affluence and cast a skeptical eye on conservation as a basis for national energy policy.

. . . During our campaign, then-Governor Bush and I spoke of energy as a storm cloud forming over the economy. America's reliance on energy, and fossil fuels in particular, has lately taken on an urgency not felt since the late 1970s. . . .

. . . Throughout the country, we've seen sharp increases in fuel prices, from home heating oil to gasoline. . . . Energy costs as a share of household expenses have been rising, and families are really feeling the pinch. . . .

Dick Cheney, Speech, 30 Apr. 2001, http://usinfo.state.gov/topical/global/energy/01043001.htm.

The crisis we face is largely the result of short-sighted domestic policies—or, as in recent years, no policy at all.

As a country, we have demanded more and more energy. But we have not brought online the supplies needed to meet that demand. . . .

In January, [President Bush] directed me to form a task force to recommend a new national energy strategy. . . . There will be many recommendations—some obvious, some more complicated. But they will all arise from three basic principles.

First, our strategy will be comprehensive in approach, and long term in outlook. By comprehensive, I mean just that—a realistic assessment of where we are, where we need to go, and what it will take. By long term, I mean none of the usual quick fixes, which in the field of energy never fix anything. Price controls, tapping strategic reserves, creating new federal agencies—if these were any solution, we'd have resolved the problems a long time ago.

. . . Years down the road, alternative fuels may become a great deal more plentiful. But we are not yet in any position to stake our economy and our own way of life on that possibility. For now, we must take the facts as they are. Whatever our hopes for developing alternative sources and for conserving energy, the reality is that fossil fuels supply virtually a hundred percent of our transportation needs, and an overwhelming share of our electricity requirements. For years down the road, this will continue to be true.

We know that in the next two decades, our country's demand for oil will grow by a third. Yet we are producing less oil today—39 percent less—than we were in 1970. We make up the difference with imports, relying ever more on the good graces of foreign suppliers. . . . Think of this: During the Arab oil embargo of the '70s, 36 percent of our oil came from abroad. Today it's 56 percent, growing steadily, and under the current trend is set to reach 64 percent less than two decades from now.

Here's what we know about natural gas. By 2020, our demand will rise by two-thirds. This is a plentiful, clean-burning fuel, and we're producing and using more of it than ever. What we have not done is build all of the needed infrastructure to carry it from the source to the user.

Then there is the energy we take most for granted, electricity. We all speak of the new economy and its marvels, sometimes forgetting that it all runs on electricity. And overall demand for electric power is expected to rise by 43 percent over the next 20 years.

So this is where we are with the demand for oil and gas and electricity. The options left to us are limited and they are clear.

For the oil we need, unless we choose to accept our growing dependence on foreign suppliers—and all that goes with that—we must increase domestic production from known sources. . . .

For the natural gas we need, we must lay more pipelines—at least 38,000 miles more—as well as many thousands of miles of added distribution lines to bring natural gas into our homes and workplaces.

For the electricity we need, we must be ambitious. Transmission grids stand in need of repair, upgrading, and expansion. . . .

. . . Over the next 20 years, just meeting projected demand will require between 1,300 and 1,900 new power plants. . . .

. . . Coal is still the most plentiful source of affordable energy in this country, and it is by far the primary source of electric power generation. This will be the case for years to come. To try and tell ourselves otherwise is to deny blunt reality.

Coal is not the cleanest source of energy, and we must support efforts to improve clean-coal technology to soften its impact on the environment.

That leads me to the second principle of our energy strategy: Good stewardship.

We will insist on protecting and enhancing the environment, showing consideration for the air and natural lands and watersheds of our country.

This will require overcoming what is for some a cherished myth—that energy production and the environment must always involve competing values. We can explore for energy, we can produce energy and use it, and we can do so with a decent regard for the natural environment.

Alaska is the best case in point. . . .

. . . In Prudhoe Bay, the vast majority of drilling over the past decade has been horizontal, allowing much oil production to go literally unnoticed, and habitat undisturbed.

The same sensitivity, and the same methods, would be applied in the event we opened production in the Arctic National Wildlife Reserve. . . . The notion that somehow developing the resources in ANWR requires a vast despoiling of the environment is provably false. . . .

We can also safeguard the environment by making greater use of the cleanest methods of power generation we know. We have, after all, mastered one form of technology that causes zero emissions of greenhouse gases, and that is nuclear power. . . . If we're serious about environmental protection, then we must seriously question the wisdom of backing away from what is, as a matter of record, a safe, clean, and very plentiful energy source. . . .

Another part of our energy future is power from renewable sources. . . . There's been progress in the use of biomass, geothermal, wind, and solar energy. Twenty years from now, with continued advances in R&D, we can reasonably expect renewables to meet three times the share of energy needs they meet today. . . .

The third and final principle of our energy strategy is to make better use, through the latest technology, of what we take from the earth. . . .

Here we aim to continue a path of uninterrupted progress in many fields. We have millions of fuel-efficient cars, where silicon chips effectively tune the engine between every firing of a spark plug. . . . Everything from light bulbs to appliances to video equipment is far more energy-efficient than ever before. New technologies are proving that we can save energy without sacrificing our standard of living. And we're going to encourage it in every way possible.

. . . The aim here is efficiency, not austerity. We all remember the energy crisis of the 1970s, when people in positions of responsibility complained that Americans just used too much energy.

Well, it's a good thing to conserve energy in our daily lives, and probably all of us can think of ways to do so. We can certainly think of ways that other people can conserve energy. And therein lies a temptation for policymakers—the impulse to begin telling Americans that we live too well, and—to recall a '70s phrase—that we've got to "do more with less." Already some groups are suggesting that government step in to force Americans to consume less energy, as if we could simply conserve or ration our way out of the situation we're in.

To speak exclusively of conservation is to duck the tough issues. Conservation may be a sign of personal virtue, but it is not a sufficient basis for a sound, comprehensive energy policy. People work very hard to get where they are. And the hardest working are the least likely to go around squandering energy, or anything else that costs them money. Our strategy will recognize that the present crisis does not represent a failing of the American people.

America's energy challenges are serious, but they are not perplexing. We know what needs to be done. We've always had the ability. We still have the resources. And, as of one hundred days ago, we once again have the leadership.

33

RALPH NADER

Dick Cheney and Conservation

May 1, 2001

Ralph Nader, the nation's leading consumer advocate, ran for president in 2000 on the Green party ticket. He responded critically to Cheney's energy policies in 2001.

Vice President Dick Cheney is a dinosaur living in the age of mammals. Imagine a public official uttering the following:

> Conservation may be a sign of personal virtue, but it is not a sufficient basis for a sound, comprehensive energy policy.
> We . . . safeguard the environment by making greater use of the cleanest methods of power generation we know . . . that is nuclear power.
> The notion that somehow developing the resources in ANWR [Arctic National Wildlife Reserve] requires a vast despoiling of the environment is provably false.

It is time for the American people to insist Mr. Cheney stop talking nonsense and to tell Mr. Cheney and his fellow "oil man" President Bush that they have to wean themselves from the economically and environmentally costly energy policies that keep taxpayers, consumers and environmentalists hooked on oil, coal and nuclear power.

Federal policy over the past century has largely failed to promote an energy system based on safe, secure, economically affordable, and environmentally benign energy sources. The tax code, budget appropriations, and regulatory processes overwhelmingly have been used to subsidize dependence on fossil fuels and nuclear power. The result: increased sickness and premature deaths, depleted family budgets, acid rain destruction of lakes, forests, and crops, oil spill contamination, polluted rivers and loss of aquatic species and the long-term peril

Ralph Nader, "Dick Cheney and Conservation," 1 May 2001, http://www/nader.org/interest/050101.html.

of climate change and radioactive waste dumps—not to mention a dependency on external energy supplies.

There is an alternative. Three decades of detailed assessments, on-the-ground results, and research and development innovations in the energy-consuming devices used in our buildings, vehicles and industries undeniably show that energy efficiency and renewable energy technologies are superior energy options for society. They offer a present and future path that is economically attractive, safe and secure from large-scale or long-term risks or threats to public health, future generations, and the environment.

But embarking on that path requires overcoming the power of the oil, nuclear and other conventional fuel industries to which both the Republicans and Democrats are indentured. Under the thumb of the dirty fuel industries, Congress and the Executive branch have refused to adopt even the most modest, common sense measures. For example, when the President's Committee of Advisors on Science and Technology concluded in a 1997 report that doubling the Department of Energy's efficiency R&D funding would produce a 40 to 1 return on the investment for the nation, Congress responded by proposing deep cuts in the efficiency and renewables R&D budgets.

The Clinton/Gore Administration nod to increased energy efficiency relied largely on corporate welfare. Rather than push for an increase in auto fuel-efficiency standards, the Administration established the Partnership for a New Generation of Vehicles (PNGV). PNGV is a $1.5 billion subsidy program for the Big Three auto companies that has done nothing to improve auto fuel efficiency but has served as a convenient smokescreen behind which the industry has been able to fend off new regulatory requirements for more efficient cars.

Energy Innovations: A Prosperous Path to a Clean Environment, a joint study prepared by half a dozen of the nation's prominent energy and environmental research and advocacy groups, shows that a handful of simple and straightforward measures could produce a significant reduction in sulfur dioxide (SO_2) emissions (prime cause of acid rain) by 2010, compared to 1990 levels, and nitrogen oxide (NO_x) emissions (a key precursor of ground-level ozone, smog) as well as deep cuts in emissions of other damaging pollutants, including fine particles, toxic metals like mercury and hydrocarbons, and carbon dioxide (CO_2) emissions.

President Bush could establish the United States as the model for other countries by adopting a sustainable energy policy that includes:

—Ending fossil fuel and nuclear corporate welfare supports, including numerous special tax preferences.

—Launching a robust federal research and development program in sustainable renewable energy sources, so that the energy-independence promises of wind, solar and other forms of renewable energy are finally realized.

—Increasing auto fuel efficiency standards (at least to 45 miles per gallon for cars and 35 miles per gallon for light trucks, to be phased in over five years) during a transition period to zero-emissions cars.

—Adopting stronger efficiency standards for appliances and mandatory energy performance building codes.

—Ensuring electricity policies which promote efficient use of electricity through a range of measures including "net metering" requirements that companies pay market prices for electricity generated by consumers and passed back to the utility and elimination of clean air exemptions for "grandfathered" fossil fuel facilities.

—Establishing a well-funded employee transition assistance fund and job-retraining program for displaced coal miners, easily affordable with the savings from greater energy efficiency.

Our country has more problems than it deserves and more solutions than it uses. It is time for the United States to stop letting Exxon-Mobil, Peabody Coal and Westinghouse shape our energy policy and for our misguided elected officials to adopt an energy strategy based on clean renewable energy and conservation. Future generations will thank us for curbing our fossil fuel appetite.

34

JIMMY CARTER

Misinformation and Scare Tactics

May 17, 2001

In this op-ed piece in the Washington Post, *the former president responded to Cheney's attack on his commitment to conservation by criticizing what he saw as the Bush-Cheney administration's unbalanced energy policy.*

It has been more than 20 years since our country developed a comprehensive energy policy. It is important for President Bush and Congress to take another look at this important issue, but not based on misleading statements made lately by high administration officials. These comments have distorted history and future needs.

I was governor of Georgia during the administration of Richard Nixon, when a combination of oil shortages and an OPEC boycott produced a real energy crisis in the United States. Five years later, the Iran-Iraq war shut off 4 million barrels of the world's daily oil supplies almost overnight, and the price of energy more than doubled in just 12 months. This caused a wave of inflation in all industrialized countries and created energy shortages. As before, there were long lines of vehicles at service stations, with drivers eager to pay even astronomical prices for available fuel.

No energy crisis exists now that equates in any way with those we faced in 1973 and 1979. World supplies are adequate and reasonably stable, price fluctuations are cyclical, reserves are plentiful, and automobiles aren't waiting in line at service stations. Exaggerated claims seem designed to promote some long-frustrated ambitions of the oil industry at the expense of environmental quality.

Also contrary to recent statements by top officials, a bipartisan Congress worked closely with me for four years to create a well-balanced approach to the problem. No influential person ever spoke "exclusively of conservation," and my administration never believed

Jimmy Carter, "Misinformation and Scare Tactics," *Washington Post,* 17 May 2001, A3.

that "we could simply conserve or ration our way out of" any energy crisis. On the contrary, we emphasized both energy conservation and the increased production of oil, gas, coal and solar energy. Permanent laws were laboriously hammered out that brought an unprecedented commitment to efficient use of energy supplies. We mandated improved home insulation, energy savings in the design of industrial equipment and home appliances and a step-by-step increase in gas mileage of all automobiles manufactured in our country.

When I was inaugurated, American vehicles were averaging only 12 miles per gallon. Today, new cars reach more than twice this gas mileage, which would be much higher except for the failure to maintain the efficiency standards, beginning in the Reagan years. (Gas mileage has actually gone down during the past five years.)

Official statistics published by the departments of energy and labor reveal the facts: Since I signed the final energy bills in 1980, America's gross national product has increased by 90 percent, while total energy consumption went up only 26 percent. Our emphasis on coal and other sources of energy and improved efficiency has limited petroleum consumption to an increase of only 12 percent. During this time, non-energy prices have risen 2½ times as much as energy prices, and gasoline prices have actually declined by 41 percent, in real terms and even including the temporary surge in the past two years.

Although these energy conservation decisions have been criticized as "a sign of [my] personal virtue," it is clear that the benefits have resulted from a commitment to improved technology, with extremely beneficial results for American consumers, business and commerce. Top executives in the oil industry should acknowledge their tremendous freedom to explore, extract and market oil and gas products that resulted from the decisions made by Congress during my term in Washington.

In fact, our most difficult legislative battle was over the deregulation of oil and gas prices, designed so that competitive prices would both discourage the waste of energy and promote exploration for new sources of petroleum products. At the end of 1980, every available drilling rig in the United States was being utilized at full capacity, and dependence on foreign imports was falling rapidly.

Despite these facts, some officials are using misinformation and scare tactics to justify such environmental atrocities as drilling in the Arctic National Wildlife Refuge. The Alaska National Interest Lands Conservation Act, which I signed in December 1980, approved 100 percent of the offshore areas and 95 percent of the potentially productive oil and mineral areas for exploration or for drilling. We excluded the wildlife refuge, confirming a decision first made by President Dwight Eisenhower, when Alaska became a state in 1959, to set aside this area as a precious natural heritage.

Those who advocate drilling in the Arctic National Wildlife Refuge to meet current needs are careful to conceal the fact that almost none of the electricity in energy-troubled California is generated from oil.

It is important for private citizens and organizations to know the facts and to join in the coming debates—so we can continue the policies of the late 1970s: a careful balance between production and conservation.

35

THOMAS L. FRIEDMAN

A Failure to Imagine

May 19, 2002

Thomas L. Friedman, a Pulitzer Prize–winning columnist for the New York Times, *often focuses on the intersection of globalization politics, economics, and international relations. In this column, he raised issues about the connections between energy policy, domestic politics, and national security.*

If you ask me, the press has this whole story about whether President Bush had a warning of a possible attack before 9/11, and didn't share it, upside down.

The failure to prevent Sept. 11 was not a failure of intelligence or coordination. It was a failure of imagination. Even if all the raw intelligence signals had been shared among the FBI, the CIA and the White House, I'm convinced that there was no one there who would have put them all together, who would have imagined evil on the scale Osama

Thomas L. Friedman, "A Failure to Imagine," *The New York Times,* 19 May 2002, sec. 4, p. 15.

bin Laden did. Osama bin Laden was (or is) a unique character. He's a combination of Charles Manson and Jack Welch[1]—a truly evil, twisted personality, but with the organizational skills of a top corporate manager, who translated his evil into a global campaign that rocked a superpower. In some ways, I'm glad that America (outside Hollywood) is not full of people with bin Laden–like imaginations. One Timothy McVeigh[2] is enough.

Imagining evil of this magnitude simply does not come naturally to the American character, which is why, even after we are repeatedly confronted with it, we keep reverting to our natural, naively optimistic selves. Because our open society is so much based on trust, and that trust is so hard-wired into the American character and citizenry, we can't get rid of it—even when we so obviously should.

So someone drives a truck bomb into the U.S. embassy in Beirut, and we still don't really protect the Marine barracks there from a similar, but much bigger, attack a few months later. Someone blows up two U.S. embassies in East Africa with truck bombs, and we still don't imagine that someone would sail an exploding dinghy into a destroyer, the USS *Cole,* a few years later. Someone tries to blow up the World Trade Center in 1993 with a truck bomb, and the guy who did it tells us he had also wanted to slam a plane into the CIA, but we still couldn't imagine someone doing just that to the Twin Towers on 9/11.

So I don't fault the president for not having imagined evil of this magnitude. But given the increasingly lethal nature of terrorism, we are going to have to adapt. We need an "Office of Evil," whose job would be to constantly sift all intelligence data and imagine what the most twisted mind might be up to.

No, I don't blame President Bush at all for his failure to imagine evil. I blame him for something much worse: his failure to imagine good.

I blame him for squandering all the positive feeling in America after 9/11, particularly among young Americans who wanted to be drafted for a great project that would strengthen America in some lasting way—a Manhattan project for energy independence. Such a project could have enlisted young people in a national movement for greater conservation and enlisted science and industry in a crash effort to produce enough renewable energy, efficiencies and domestic production to wean us gradually off oil imports.

[1]In August 1969, Charles Manson led a cult that killed seven people in California. Jack Welch was the forceful CEO of General Electric from 1981 to 2001.

[2]Timothy McVeigh was convicted of killing 168 people in the April 19, 1995, bombing of the Murrah Federal Building in Oklahoma City.

Such a project would not only have made us safer by making us independent of countries who share none of our values. It would also have made us safer by giving the world a much stronger reason to support our war on terrorism. There is no way we can be successful in this war without partners, and there is no way America will have lasting partners, especially in Europe, unless it is perceived as being the best global citizen it can be. And the best way to start conveying that would be by reducing our energy gluttony and ratifying the Kyoto treaty to reduce global warming.

President Bush is not alone in this failure. He has had the full cooperation of the Democratic party leadership, which has been just as lacking in imagination. This has made it easy for Mr. Bush, and his oil-industry paymasters, to get away with it.

We and our kids are going to regret this. Because a war on terrorism that is fought only by sending soldiers to Afghanistan or by tightening our borders will ultimately be unsatisfying. Such a war is important, but it can never be definitively won. Someone will always slip through. But a war on terrorism that, with some imagination, is broadly defined as making America safer by also making it better is a war that could be won. It's a war that could ensure that something lasting comes out of 9/11, other than longer lines at the airport—and that something would be enhanced respect for America and a country and a planet that would be greener, cleaner and safer in the broadest sense.

Too bad we don't have a president who could imagine that.

A Chronology of Events Surrounding the Energy Crisis of the 1970s (1973–1981)

1973

April 18 Richard Nixon calls for an end to oil import quotas, warning Americans of upcoming energy shortages and rising gas prices.

October 6 Yom Kippur War begins when Syria and Egypt attack Israel.

October 17 Objecting to U.S. support of Israel, Arab states ban export of oil to United States. Price of oil rises more than 350 percent.

November 7 Nixon calls on nation to reduce use of energy.

November 16 Nixon signs bill to build Trans-Alaskan Pipeline.

November 19 Senate passes National Energy Emergency Act, authorizing Nixon to require adoption of conservation measures.

1974

August 9 Nixon resigns; Gerald Ford is sworn in as president.

Fall Ford launches Whip Inflation Now! (WIN!) program, which is not successful in controlling prices. In 1974–75, United States experiences worst recession since 1930s.

1975

January 3 Ford signs Trade Reform Act, barring OPEC nations from tariff benefits given to other countries.

October 20 End of five-year agreement with USSR to trade U.S. grain for oil, causing increased dependence on OPEC oil.

1977

January 20 Inauguration of Jimmy Carter as thirty-ninth president.

January 21 Carter calls on Americans to set their thermostats no higher than 65°F to alleviate oil shortage.

April 18 Carter addresses the nation, calling the energy crisis the "moral equivalent of war."

August 4 Creation of Department of Energy.

1978

September Shah is unable to quell massive riots in Iran.

September 5–17 Carter mediates peace agreement between Egypt and Israel at Camp David.

October 15 Congress passes an energy package, first successful attempt at a unified policy.

December 17 Oil price increases planned by OPEC.

December 27 Iran ceases exporting oil.

1979

February 1 Ayatollah Khomeini returns to Iran from exile.

March 28 Nuclear reactor incident at Three Mile Island, near Harrisburg, Pennsylvania, shakes public's faith in atomic power.

April 5 Carter addresses the nation on energy, saying he will lift price controls on gas and calling for a windfall profits tax.

June Many states institute odd/even-day rationing rules for buying gas. Lines lengthen at gas stations. Truckers strike begins.

June 18 In Vienna, Carter signs SALT II treaty with Leonid Brezhnev of USSR.

June 29 At Tokyo summit, world's industrial nations put ceilings on oil imports to pressure OPEC to reduce oil prices.

July 1 Carter slips behind Reagan and Ford in the polls, as voters grow angry and frustrated over gasoline shortages. Carter returns from trip to Europe and Asia.

July 4 Carter cancels his July 5 address to the nation.

July 6 Lines at gas stations become shorter, and gasoline prices stabilize. Carter begins a series of meetings at Camp David.

July 9 Saudi Arabia promises to increase oil output. Congress agrees to consider Carter's energy plan, but only if public thinks there is a crisis.

July 10 Carter signs proclamation that air-conditioning in public buildings should be set no lower than 78°F and announces that price controls on gas will not be removed, increasing fears of higher prices.

July 11 Camp David talks end.

July 15 Carter delivers "crisis of confidence" speech.

July 16 Carter travels and gives more speeches, rallying support. Congressional Democrats are supportive; Republicans are skeptical.

July 17 Carter's approval rating increases to 37 percent, up 11 points. Cabinet members hand in their resignations, with firings and forced resignations following. Carter approval rating decreases.

November 4 American hostages seized at U.S. embassy in Iran.

November 7 Democratic senator Edward M. Kennedy enters race for the presidency.

1980

January 23 Carter issues "Carter Doctrine": To protect national security interests, the United States will use military force against any attempt by a hostile nation seeking control of the Persian Gulf.

June 6 Congress overrides a presidential veto, ending the $4.62 per barrel fee on imported oil.

September 22 Iran-Iraq War begins.

November 4 Republican Ronald Reagan defeats Carter in presidential election.

1981

January 20 Iranian hostage crisis is resolved; hostages are released. Inauguration of Reagan as fortieth president.

Questions for Consideration

1. Do you think Carter had an accurate view of America as a self-indulgent and narcissistic society shaped by an excessive pursuit of consumer pleasures?

2. In the debates within the Carter administration between Patrick Caddell and Walter Mondale, which side had the more convincing and politically astute position?

3. As Carter drafted his July 15, 1979, speech, what kinds of choices did he make and what lay behind his choices?

4. In a situation like the one the nation faced in 1979, what should be the role of morality and religious beliefs in shaping national policy?

5. How did different groups respond to Carter's speech and why?

6. What role did considerations of events in the Middle East (protection of oil supplies and Israel's security, for example) play in deliberations about domestic policy? Do you think this was appropriate?

7. What were the strengths and weaknesses of Carter's presidential leadership?

8. How would you assess Carter's decision to use ideas offered by intellectuals to shape public policy at a critical moment in his presidency?

9. On what grounds did Ted Kennedy and Ronald Reagan take issue with Carter's approach?

10. What lessons can the nation learn from the events of the summer of 1979?

Selected Bibliography

GENERAL BACKGROUND OF THE 1970S

Bernstein, Michael A., and David E. Adler, eds. *Understanding American Economic Decline.* Cambridge: Cambridge University Press, 1994.

Bluestone, Barry, and Bennett Harrison. *The Deindustrialization of America: Plant Closings, Community Abandonment, and the Dismantling of American Industry.* New York: Basic Books, 1982.

Burnham, Walter Dean. *The Current Crisis in American Politics.* New York: Oxford University Press, 1982.

Carroll, Peter N. *It Seemed Like Nothing Happened: America in the 1970s.* New Brunswick, N.J.: Rutgers University Press, 1984.

Crawford, Allan. *Thunder on the Right: The "New Right" and the Politics of Resentment.* New York: Pantheon, 1980.

Edsall, Thomas Byrne, with Mary D. Edsall. *Chain Reaction: The Impact of Race, Rights, and Taxes on American Politics.* New York: Norton, 1991.

Riechley, A. James. *Conservatives in an Age of Change: The Nixon and Ford Administrations.* Washington, D.C.: Brookings Institution, 1981.

Sale, Kirkpatrick. *Power Shift: The Rise of the Southern Rim and Its Challenge to the Eastern Establishment.* New York: Random House, 1975.

Schulman, Bruce J. *The Seventies: The Great Shift in American Culture, Society, and Politics.* New York: Free Press, 2001.

JIMMY CARTER AND THE CARTER PRESIDENCY

Bourne, Peter G. *Jimmy Carter: A Comprehensive Biography from Plains to Postpresidency.* New York: Scribner, 1997.

Brinkley, Douglas. *The Unfinished Presidency: Jimmy Carter's Journey Beyond the White House.* New York: Viking, 1998.

Carter, Jimmy. *An Hour Before Daylight: Memories of a Rural Boyhood.* New York: Simon & Schuster, 2001.

Carter, Jimmy. *Keeping Faith: Memoirs of a President.* New York: Bantam, 1982.

Carter, Rosalynn. *First Lady from Plains.* Boston: Houghton Mifflin, 1984.

189

Drumbrell, John. *The Carter Presidency.* Manchester, England: Manchester University Press, 1993.

Fallows, James. "The Passionless Presidency." *Atlantic Monthly,* May 1979, 33–48, and June 1979, 75–81.

Fink, Gary M., and Hugh Davis Graham, eds. *The Carter Presidency: Policy Choices in the Post-New Deal Era.* Lawrence: University Press of Kansas, 1998. Especially John C. Barrow, "An Age of Limits: Jimmy Carter and the Quest for a National Energy Policy," 158–78.

Gillon, Steven M. *The Democrats' Dilemma: Walter F. Mondale and the Liberal Legacy.* New York: Columbia University Press, 1992.

Glad, Betty. *Jimmy Carter: In Search of the Great White House.* New York: Norton, 1980.

Hargrove, Erwin C. *Jimmy Carter as President.* Baton Rouge: Louisiana State University Press, 1988.

Hertzberg, Hendrik. "Jimmy Carter, 1977–1981." In *Character Above All: Ten Presidents from FDR to George Bush,* ed. Robert A. Wilson, 190–94. New York: Simon & Schuster, 1995.

Jones, Charles O. *The Trustee Presidency: Jimmy Carter and the United States Congress.* Baton Rouge: Louisiana State University Press, 1988.

Kaufman, Burton I. *The Presidency of James Earl Carter, Jr.* Lawrence: University Press of Kansas, 1993.

Morris, Kenneth E. *Jimmy Carter: American Moralist.* Athens: University of Georgia Press, 1996.

Nielsen, N. C. *The Religion of President Carter.* London: Mowbrays, 1977.

Ribuffo, Leo P. "God and Jimmy Carter." In *Right Left Center: Essays in American History,* 214–48. New Brunswick, N.J.: Rutgers University Press, 1992.

Rosenbaum, Herbert D., and Alexej Ugrinsky, eds. *Jimmy Carter: Foreign Policy and Post-Presidential Years.* Westport, Conn.: Greenwood Press, 1994.

Rosenbaum, Herbert D., and Alexej Ugrinsky, eds. *The Presidency and Domestic Policies of Jimmy Carter.* Westport, Conn.: Greenwood Press, 1994.

Schoenbaum, David. *The United States and the State of Israel.* New York: Oxford University Press, 1993.

Smith, Charles D. *Palestine and the Arab-Israeli Conflict.* 4th ed. Boston: Bedford/St. Martin's, 2001.

CARTER'S SPEECH OF JULY 15, 1979

Drew, Elizabeth. "A Reporter at Large: Phase—In Search of a Definition." *New Yorker,* 27 Aug. 1979, 45–46, 49–50, 53–54, 56, 59–60, 63–64, and 66–73.

Hahn, Dan F. "Flailing the Profligate: Carter's Energy Sermon of 1979." *Political Science Quarterly,* 10 (Fall 1980): 583–87.

Holland, J. William. "The Great Gamble: Jimmy Carter and the 1979 Energy Crisis." *Prologue,* 22 (Spring 1990): 63–79.

Kramer, Scott. "Struggles of an Outsider: The 1979 Energy Crisis and President Carter's Call for Confidence." Senior thesis, Department of History, Princeton University, 1992.

Ribuffo, Leo. "'Malaise' Revisited: Jimmy Carter and the Crisis of Confidence." In *The Liberal Persuasion: Arthur Schlesinger, Jr., and the Challenge of the American Past,* ed. John Patrick Diggins, 164–84. Princeton, N.J.: Princeton University Press, 1997.

Strong, Robert A. "Reclaiming Leadership: The Carter Administration and the Crisis of Confidence." *Political Science Quarterly,* 16 (Fall 1986): 636–50.

OIL, POLITICS, AND DIPLOMACY

Calleo, David P. *The Imperious Economy.* Cambridge: Harvard University Press, 1982.

Melosi, Martin V. *Coping with Abundance: Energy and Environment in Industrial America.* New York: Knopf, 1985.

Smith, Gaddis. *Morality, Reason, and Power: American Diplomacy in the Carter Years.* New York: Hill and Wang, 1986.

Tugwell, Franklin. *The Energy Crisis and the American Political Economy: Politics and Markets in the Management of Natural Resources.* Stanford, Calif.: Stanford University Press, 1988.

Yergin, Daniel. *The Prize: The Epic Quest for Oil, Money, and Power.* New York: Simon & Schuster, 1991.

DEBATES ABOUT POLITICS, IDEAS, AND SOCIETY

Collins, Robert M. *More: The Politics of Economic Growth in Postwar America.* New York: Oxford University Press, 2000.

Fukuyama, Francis. *The Great Disruption: Human Nature and the Reconstruction of Social Order.* New York: Free Press, 1999.

Gilder, George. *Wealth and Poverty.* New York: Basic Books, 1981.

Hays, Samuel P. *Beauty, Health and Permanence.* New York: Cambridge University Press, 1987.

Heilbroner, Robert L. *An Inquiry into the Human Prospect.* New York: Norton, 1974.

Hirsch, Fred. *Social Limits to Growth.* Cambridge: Harvard University Press, 1976.

Horowitz, Daniel. *The Anxieties of Affluence: Critiques of American Consumer Culture, 1939–1979.* Amherst: University of Massachusetts Press, 2004.

Leiss, William. *Limits to Satisfaction: An Essay on the Problems of Needs and Commodities.* Toronto: Toronto University Press, 1976.

Marsden, George M. *Understanding Fundamentalism and Evangelicalism.* Grand Rapids, Mich.: Eerdmans, 1991.

Ophuls, William. *Ecology and the Politics of Scarcity: Prologue to a Political Theory of the Steady State.* San Francisco: Freeman, 1977.

Schnall, Maxine. *Limits: A Search for New Values.* New York: Clarkson N. Potter, 1981.

Shi, David E. *The Simple Life: Plain Living and High Thinking in American Culture.* New York: Oxford University Press, 1985.

Thurow, Lester C. *The Zero-Sum Society: Distribution and the Possibilities for Economic Change.* New York: Basic Books, 1980.

Wolfe, Alan. *America's Impasse: The Rise and Fall of the Politics of Growth.* New York: Pantheon, 1981.

Wolfe, Tom. "The Me Decade and the Third Great Awakening." In *The Purple Decades,* 265–93. New York: Farrar, Straus and Giroux, 1982.

WEB RESOURCES

"Jimmy Carter." *American Experience.* Two-hour special on Jimmy Carter, which includes footage on his "crisis of confidence" speech. http://www.pbs.org/wgbh/amex/carter.

Jimmy Carter Presidential Library and Museum. http://www.jimmycarterlibrary.org.

ACKNOWLEDGMENTS

Document 2. David Stockman, "The Wrong War? The Case against a National Energy Policy." Reprinted with the permission of the author from *The Public Interest,* No. 53 (Fall 1978), pp. 3–44, © 1978 by National Affairs, Inc.

Document 3. Tom Morgenthau, with John Walcott, Thomas M. DeFrank, Lea Donosky, and Holly Morris, "The Energy Plague." From *Newsweek,* July 2, 1979, © 1979 Newsweek, Inc. All rights reserved. Reprinted by permission.

Document 4. "Carter on the *Titanic.*" © 1979 by National Review, Inc., 215 Lexington Avenue, New York, NY 10016. Reprinted by permission.

Document 5. Alexis de Tocqueville, *Democracy in America.* From *Democracy in America* by Alexis de Tocqueville, translated by Henry Reeve, copyright 1945 and renewed 1973 by Alfred A. Knopf, a division of Random House, Inc. Used by permission of Alfred A. Knopf, a division of Random House, Inc.

Document 7. Christopher Lasch, *The Culture of Narcissism.* "Preface," from *The Culture of Narcissism: American Life in an Age of Diminishing Expectations* by Christopher Lasch. Copyright © 1991 by Christopher Lasch. Used by Permission of W. W. Norton & Company, Inc.

Document 8. Robert Bellah, "Human Conditions for a Good Society." Reprinted with permission of the *St. Louis Post-Dispatch,* copyright 1979.

Document 13. Walter Mondale, "Energy Speech: Memo to the President." Reprinted with permission of the author.

Document 14. Marshall Loeb, "How to Counter OPEC." © 1979 TIME Inc. Reprinted by permission.

Document 19. "The Real Jimmy Carter." Reprinted with permission of *The Wall Street Journal* © 1979. Dow Jones Company, Inc. All rights reserved.

Document 20. "Gantry on Energy." © 1979 by National Review, Inc., 215 Lexington Avenue, New York, NY 10016. Reprinted by permission.

Document 21. "Carter's Crisis — and Ours." Reprinted by permission from *The Progressive,* 409 E. Main St., Madison, WI 53703; www.progressive.org.

Document 22. "Coming to Grips with the Energy Crisis." Reprinted with permission of the AFL-CIO.

Document 23. Theodore A. Snyder Jr., "Our Energy Future—A Time to Choose." Reprinted with permission from *Sierra.*

Document 24. "Two Cheers for a Start." Reprinted with permission from *The Jewish Week* of New York.

Document 25. "Energy Sermon." Reprinted with permission from *America.*

Document 26. "Christians Should Lead in Conservation." Reprinted with permission from *Christian Index.*

Document 28. Robert Bellah, "A Night at Camp David." Reprinted with permission of the author, Professor of Sociology Emeritus, University of California, Berkeley, and coauthor of *Habits of the Heart: Individualism and Commitment in American Life* (1980).

Document 29. Christopher Lasch, "Letter to Patrick Caddell." Reprinted with permission of Nell Lasch.

Document 30. Edward M. Kennedy, "Speech." Reprinted with permission of the author.

Document 31. Ronald Reagan, "A Vision for America." Reprinted with permission of the Office of Ronald Reagan.

Document 33. Ralph Nader, "Dick Cheney and Conservation." Reprinted with permission of the author, Consumer Advocate Center.

Document 34. Jimmy Carter, "Misinformation and Scare Tactics." Reprinted with permission of the author.

Document 35. Thomas L. Friedman, "A Failure to Imagine." Originally published in *The New York Times,* May 19, 2002.

Index